flowerpots

jim keeling

flowerpots

a seasonal guide to designing and planting container gardens

jim keeling

photography by andrew lawson

kyle cathie ltd

First published in Great Britain 2004 by
Kyle Cathie Limited
122 Arlington Road
London NW1 7HP
general.enquiries@kyle-cathie.com
www.kylecathie.com

10 9 8 7 6 5 4 3 2 1

ISBN 1 85626 490 4

Senior Editor Muna Reyal
Designer Geoff Hayes
Photographer Andrew Lawson
Copy editor Karen Collier
Editorial assistant Jennifer Wheatley
Proofreader Galiena Hitchman
Index Helen Snaith
Production Sha Huxtable

A Cataloguing In Publication record for this title is
available from the British Library.

Colour reproduction by Colourscan
Printed and bound in Singapore by Tien-Wah Press

Nothing that comes out of Whichford Pottery is a lone effort, and
this book is no exception. It would still be just a pale shadow, but
for the help and support given me in many ways: in particular,
Isobel Pinfold and Harriet Rycroft for their practical gardening and
literary flair; Niki Bennet for her informed reading; Rosie Fairfax-
Cholmeley for her research; Muna Reyal, my editor, and the Kyle
Cathie team for their patient support and encouragement; Sue
Dickinson, Kathy Brown, Paul Williams, Fergus Garrett and
Christopher Lloyd for their brilliant horticultural contributions; my
office (especially Jane Lanciault), family and friends for ploughing
through endless scruffy redrafts; Andrew Lawson for good-
humoured photography; Geoff Hayes for his excellent design;
Dominique and my family (always); and, of course, everyone at the
pottery past and present, and all the other potters down the ages,
who have helped me to where I am now.

Jim Keeling
Whichford Pottery
Whichford, Nr. Shipston-on-Stour
Warwickshire, CV36 5PG
Tel: 01608 684416
Fax: 01608 684833
email: flowerpots@whichfordpottery.com
website: www.whichfordpottery.com

Whichford POTTERY

contents

introduction

It is getting late in the afternoon and the sun is urging me to come outside. But half-finished pots surround me, waiting, impatient to be brought to final form and life. I have spent half the day discussing planting ideas for the Chelsea Flower Show; then we had a problem with the roof of the big kiln and one of the apprentices has just put the wrong sprig decoration on a whole line of pots. I am tired and not happy as I tie on my clay-stiffened apron. 'Who's got the big Whichford roulette?' I complain, 'and where's my sponge?' I turn, and there are the visitors whom I saw earlier sitting in the garden. 'What beautiful pots!' they say, pointing to the new row of misfits. Scowling, I look too. The sun is coming in low across them. They steam slightly in its heat and the newly applied sprigs stand out crisply, actually fitting the shape rather well I notice, each pot slightly different, each an individual expression of a common theme. 'What a wonderful place to work. How lucky you are!' the visitors murmur, with an almost religious hush as they watch me throwing. I ease out the shoulder on a big ali baba jar, to find the curve that grows and bends, the pressure from my fingers constantly choosing between the hundreds of paths this shape could follow, cajoling the inert clay into this most anthropomorphic of flowerpots, always one of my favourites.

My favourites. Yes: in the hurly-burly of running a busy workshop it is easy to feel swamped by the everyday pressures of life, but what the visitors say is true. Making garden pots is a very pleasing skill and making them in this valley, on the edge of the Cotswold hills, with a convivial team of fellow craftsmen and women, is as pleasurable a job as I can think of.

As I reach for my sponge to put the finishing touches to the ali baba jar, squeezing warm water out over the rim between clay-covered fingers, I look down into the afternoon garden. There I see its sister, fired orange, topped with a spray of pink-striped phormium elegantly surrounded by a ruff of purple verbena. I think of all the hundreds of other brothers, sisters and cousins that I have made, now in other gardens all over England – and indeed, the world; each dressed quite differently, each conversing with a different landscape.

Here at Whichford, our planting style is informal; a slightly rowdy party, with the guests jostling and laughing in a colourful throng, or perched for a moment's rest and reflection on some low wall. But my mind wanders to other gardens, more elegant or serious, where the dress is more restrained, sober even, and formal ranks of pots lead the eye on to some fine vista or far-off hills. And I remember courtyards and balconies, and tiny slivers of town gardens where my pots have become part of the family, tight-knit and intimate, almost sitting on your lap as you have breakfast in the summer sun.

Left: It makes no sense to talk of flowerpots without the plants that suit them.
Facing page: Autumn mists and the early morning sun lend magic to a corner of the stockyard at Whichford, all set in a Cotswold valley.

Where it all began

I have always been a gardener. I grew up surrounded by the paraphernalia of gardening, the secateurs and twine, trugs and watering cans, and those inevitable collections of odd left-hand gloves that were always lying around. When very small, I used to trail after my mother, pulling up the wrong plants. Once I watered all her potted geranium cuttings with a watering can full of prepared weedkiller. Later on, I seemed destined to spend eternities edging lawns. I would retreat to my own little plot with its broken stone path, the tiny pond which I puddled out of cement and a fishing, red-capped gnome, of which I was inordinately proud. (In my early garden design days I was unaware of the Chelsea Flower Show strictures, still in force today, banning the use of garden gnomes in show gardens!)

Then there was the potting shed. It was strategically placed at the bottom of the long, sloping Edwardian garden, the ancient realm of long-dead gardeners, dilapidated now, full of broken tools, jam jars, nameless dried-out bottles of poison and mouse-eaten seed packets. In the dirt under the workbenches lived many bundles of old flowerpots that I would stack up to make the walls of dens. Later, when I became apprenticed to a pottery which specialised in the making of flowerpots, their shapes, sizes and textures seemed, thus, already familiar to me.

And then came clay

Below the potting shed, a path led down a steep bank, still clothed with a bluebell-strewn slice of the ancient Surrey oak and elm forest. At the bottom of this was a wide old boundary ditch, always with a drift of fallen oak leaves that covered the bottom, yet still leaving steep sides six feet high cut into pure, yellow gault clay.

It was here that I first encountered the pleasures of clay. At the age of six, I opened up a small mine in the side of the ditch, and had soon excavated a shelf. I would mix the summer clay with ditch water, and beat the floor of my pit flat, burnishing it smooth before lying curled up against the damp sides like some small animal. There, I'd watch the swaying oaks, surrounded by the smell of clay.

The visitors are gone now – just as well, because I am still standing looking out at the garden, lost in these rememberings. Was I a potter or a gardener first? It is certain that both clay and earth have always drawn me to them.

School life

At my first school, Modelling and Gardening were the cups that I coveted: not for me sports or academia. Every aspect of our life at this school was regulated by a competition for a silver cup, awarded at the end of the summer term. Nowadays this is regarded as a politically suspect system for motivating small boys, but to it I owe my first endeavours of creation in clay.

My main desire was to win the Modelling Cup. How to do this, when my friend Heddon Johnson had such gifted help from his mother, quite apart from being far better than me with balsa wood? As in all serious competitive sports, there was the usual hierarchy of endeavour: start with a plastic Airfix kit of the Mayflower, gluey fingers misting any clear plastic parts, transfers awry and applied before the garish paintwork. From there, the gradual build-up in size, and, finally, premier league; try something not in kit form.

My first attempt at modelling was a balsa and plywood stagecoach about eight inches high. To mark it out from Heddon's models, I chose a new material, clay, and with it modelled four clay horses.

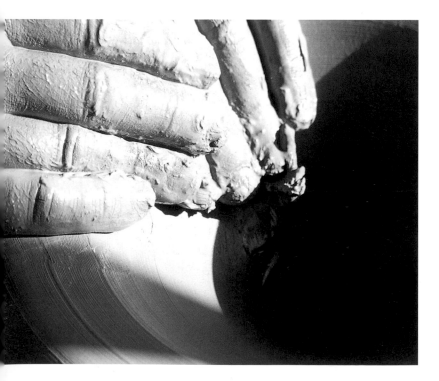

Left: Both gardening and flower-potting involve rolling up your sleeves and getting your hands dirty.
Facing page: The courtyard garden at Whichford where we are always trying out new plants and ideas.

We must have had a clay modelling department, for I remember coil pots. Alas, though, we had no kiln, and I soon learnt the impossibility of mending broken, dry, unfired clay: much glue coated with many layers of unsticky white clay from successive breaks.

After this, at the age of 12, I made a 2ft by 1ft high model of a Greek temple. You could lift the roof, painted inside in gold and dark blue, to show the clay Zeus (head separate, held in place by a wooden dowel) and small clay figurines prostrating themselves, or sacrificing to the deity. I modelled two tall pedestal urns (gold with silver swags, standing on square plinths) to put in front of the temple. With this model, I at last won the coveted cup; and by then I was hooked on making things out of clay.

My other great joy, when out of the social hurly-burly, was my garden, a 6ft by 4ft plot in the school allotments. These were run by the strict but kind Mr Truran, iron judge of the inevitable Gardening Cup (no wonder I bank my edges so precisely). But what an honour to be given a slip of plant from his immaculate garden!

Why flowerpots?

Years later, when casting around for a career at the end of my time at university, I remembered my early fascination with clay and decided to become a potter. I eventually took up an apprenticeship at the pottery nearest my parents' home, at Wrecclesham, on the Surrey-Hampshire border. Unique in England, they made, quite by chance, only flowerpots – so without any planning on my part, I ended up with a career that combined my two earliest passions.

Wrecclesham Pottery was founded in 1874 by Absalom Harris who came from a long line of itinerant Hampshire potters. By the time I arrived to learn my trade, four generations later, the pottery's days of expansion and glory were long gone and the buildings were falling down around our ears. The working conditions were from another age, both primitive and magical. Sloping earth floors led you through a labyrinth of dimly lit drying rooms, in the middle of which was a coal-fired heating flue, the only source of warmth. It was here that the other apprentice and I would huddle at tea-break, toasting sandwiches and playing cards.

On bright, frosty mornings, I arrived to a workshop filled with cold, choking smoke billowing up from coal braziers, which supposedly helped to keep the frost off the wet pots. In one of the low, dark downstairs rooms, I was set to work on an ancient kickwheel set beside a grimy window – the few electric lights were seldom used.

Absalom had been unusual for his day in that he managed to set up a thriving pottery in hard times by specialising in flowerpots. Having trained at Wrecclesham with Reginald Harris (Absalom's great-grandson) and Fred Whitbread (Reg's cousin), instead of the more usual route of learning pottery at art school, my choice was limited: flowerpots were actually all that I knew how to make – and so I followed Absalom's lead.

And finally, Whichford

In 1976, 102 years after he founded Wrecclesham, I started my own pottery, first at Middle Barton in Oxfordshire. Then, from 1982, I was at Whichford, ten miles to the north, and just across the border into Warwickshire.

Whichford Pottery is built in a field behind my house, in the centre of a small village which lies at the bottom of a wooded bank on the northern edge of the Cotswold Hills. At the far end is the raw clay – piled, weathering, waiting for refining. At the other end is a courtyard garden, with displays of planted-up pots that change with the seasons and lines of finished pots laid out for sale. In between stands the pottery itself. It looks like an old timber-framed barn complex but, in fact, it is a purpose-made pottery, built up over 20 years, and modelled on Wrecclesham. Downstairs, you have clay stores and kilns, but most of the making is done upstairs, where slatted floors above the kilns are stacked with pots drying in the waste heat coming up from below.

Back in 1974, when I was working at Wrecclesham, the bottom had already fallen out of the volume market for plain, hand-made flowerpots. This was eroded first by machine-mades then, from the early 1960s by plastic, which found favour with large-scale growers for its ease of use. It became clear to me that the areas left to hand-makers were unusual designs and very large pots. To make either of these industrially involves large capital outlay for 'tooling up', whereas a hand potter with enough skill needs only a few simple tools to create spectacular results. So the growth of

Whichford Pottery is the story of acquiring these skills and the building up of a team who share them.

It is a central part of the Whichford creed that every pot is entirely hand made, each one the responsibility of a particular maker. We all follow the same catalogue of designs and sizes; however the character of each individual maker inevitably shines through their creations, giving subtle variations to line or weight. This delights me but sometimes drives the sales team to distraction as they try to choose a dozen pots that are exactly the same for some especially finickety customer.

At the heart of our production are all the traditional specialist horticultural wares I learnt to make at Wrecclesham – the longtoms, seed pans, half pots, orchid pots, seakale and rhubarb forcers and so on. These are not just copies, but are part of an unbroken line of production stretching back hundreds of years. This is especially important when it comes to training, because these pots hold the aesthetic of the tradition in an impersonal way, and teach the fundamental relationships of form and balance that have evolved in the Western world over many hundreds of years. New designs that come out of Whichford are governed by this aesthetic. At its best, this approach should stimulate a sense of familiarity and recognition in the beholder, even if the design being looked at is, in fact, quite radically new.

Working at Whichford

Like Wrecclesham in its heyday, this is a busy place. Many pairs of hands are needed to turn the five tons of raw clay we use each week into finished and fired pots using only simple traditional techniques. There are about 30 of us working at Whichford and you will meet many of them in the chapters that follow. Richard and Brian, both born in the valley, methodically mixing our clays; apprentices Joe, Adam (my son), Robert and Liz, learning their craft; and Rachel, her eagle eye lining up complex decorations. Because there is so much talk of gardening, you will come to know our gardeners, Issy and Harriet, very well. But there are others who stay behind the scenes, skilled throwers, and packers who can molly-coddle delicate pots halfway round the world, and the office team.

To keep our craft alive, however, it is not sufficient just to be good at traditional making. We also have to be inventive where we can in

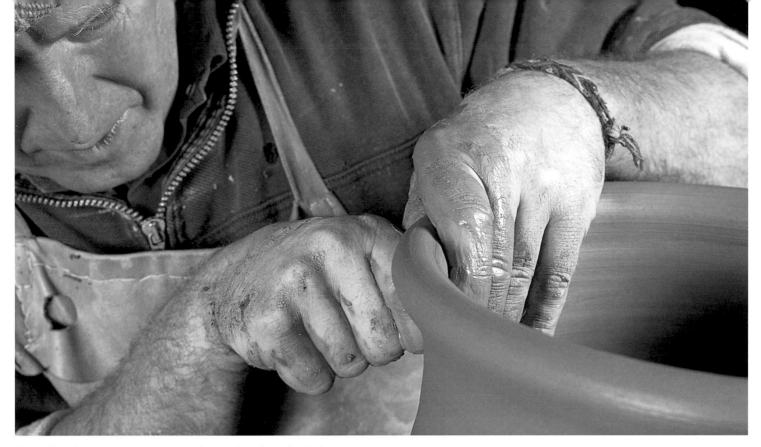

Above: Throwing requires great concentration, but is endlessly fascinating.

technique, design, use of our pots, and in how we present them. Much of our business comes by word of mouth, but a dedicated team in the office works hard making up new adverts, arranging shows around the country, keeping in touch with those on our mailing list, or putting on special events at the pottery.

I particularly enjoy these special weekends, and they often feel more like a party than a selling exercise. We are helped by the glorious location of Whichford, folded in its hills, with the pottery set back from the village road among the fields and hedges. The courtyard garden, which you will see in many photographs, spreads out in front of the pottery while, behind it, my family garden runs back towards the road and my house. It is a rambling cottage garden with many nooks and crannies that is squeezed between the various buildings in a circular garden with deep herbaceous beds. An informal lawn bumps up and down around an old dew pond overhung by pollarded willows. Off this, is a secret 'paradise' garden with high mud walls, a central raised pond and, in a gazebo to one side, a beaten-up old sofa on which to sit and look out at the dense plantings.

Each summer, all this is opened up to become the setting of a jamboree, with music and talks and picnics outside in quiet corners.

In the winter version, there are braziers outside, and chestnuts, with soup and mulled wine to warm you as you lean against the kilns. Pottery and gardening are both still bound to the old rhythms of the seasons. So to me it is natural, when I come to describe all this to you, that I should set it in that context, and my year starts, as every schoolchild knows, after the summer holidays.

Each chapter opens with a portrait of the work that we do in the pottery and then moves into the garden. They close with a plant list which is sometimes a little artificial in its choice of season – plants may choose to perform earlier or later than suggested, or may look good in other seasons too. We have, however, tried everything mentioned, and have put them into the season in which we find them most useful. Some of the perennials (including bulbs and shrubs) will be happier in the open ground after a few seasons unless repotted or at least given a good top dressing. We have only mentioned particular varieties or cultivars if we have happened to try them and liked them. Many of our plants have countless close relatives, a great number of which will be worth trying if you have the time and funds.

But I get ahead of myself. Let us begin at the beginning, on an early autumn morning, a slight nip in the air and the colours just starting to turn to gold…

autumn

Season of mists and mellow fruitfulness
     Close bosom-friend of the maturing sun;
Conspiring with him how to load and bless
     With fruit the vines that round the thatch-eaves run;
To bend with apples the moss'd cottage-trees,
     And fill all fruit with ripeness to the core;

Keats was right. There is a generosity to early autumn that fills up everything. Even the air becomes heavy with dew, and you wake to a world of glittering silver. The garden suddenly seems to be a maze of spider's webs, hung between the sparkling spikes of flowers, or laid like the waves of a frozen sea across the long meadow grasses.

Later, the battle will be slow and painful and eventually lost but, for now, the sun still has the easy strength to melt the low mists which come with the dew. This combination of water and fire in the air lends every colour a final brightness. Almost as if in response, nature fills the garden with her hottest, strongest colours – flaming reds, intense yellows and searing oranges. Even the cold blue is pulled towards purple in the bursts of Michaelmas daisies and late aconitums.

I see all of this as I open the back door and look up the path past our house towards the pottery, looming a stone's throw away. How is it that one feels almost apologetic on a day like this as one first steps outside, not wanting to disturb nature in her earliest wakings and stretchings? I close the door gently – the rest of the household is not yet awake – and pad softly out, conspiratorially sharing with all first-risen life, the heady scents of autumn.

Facing page: A scarlet solenostemon burns with autumnal intensity, the spikes of the *Phormium* 'Maori Sunrise' shooting from it like flames. It is held in place and mellowed by purple sage and heuchera, in a pot festooned with autumn fruit. Below: Late autumn frost decorates a stack of pots emptied for the winter.

And why am I up so early? Today, we begin our annual clay winning, which is the digging of a year's supply of clay. It is always wise to be at the pit to make sure that digger, driver and all understand exactly which seam is used by Whichford. Otherwise, we end up with a couple of hundred tons of useless clay or, worse still, a great many failed pots because the clay is not right.

Our main source of clay – a brickworks about eight miles away – is a vast hole in the ground towards the edge of a wide valley, with

the wooded Cotswold hills rising up behind. The clay seams there vary both vertically and horizontally, from a dark blue-grey deep in the ground, to a sandy yellow near the surface.

As I drive up the long hill south out of Whichford, thin swathes of mist rush at the car. At the top of the hill, a climb of nearly 120m (400ft), I am rewarded by the sight of the sun, still caught low in the hedges. By the time I reach the pit, its heat will have cleared all mists for the day.

These days, clay winning is a prosaic business involving large diggers and heavy lorries. Whilst it may have been more picturesque before machines, however, it was a horribly laborious process. Clay pits become almost impassable mud baths in wet weather, so digging is always done in summer or early autumn, when the clay is sullenly dry and hard.

Although clay is one of the most common substances on earth, as many of you gardeners know, it is also one of the most varied. Just as in colour it ranges from pure white to jet black, with every shade of brown, grey, yellow and even green in between, each different clay has its own distinct character, often a result of distant birth.

A clay laid down with the coal forests of the Carboniferous period, around 290 million years ago, will be stained dark with fossilised plant material, and will be sticky and dense. However, a clay derived from the fine silt of an estuary or lake will more likely be a sandy-brown colour, drier and less pliable – a little like short pastry. Pockets of glacial clay washed out during the many ice ages include the superfine and bright white kaolin china clay, much prized by the paper industry.

Left: Whichford is set in a wooded valley on the edge of the Cotswolds, and the landscape is a constant source of inspiration.
Facing page: When it is dry, clay is like a soft rock: potters witness the dramatic transformations that water and, later, fire work on its nature.

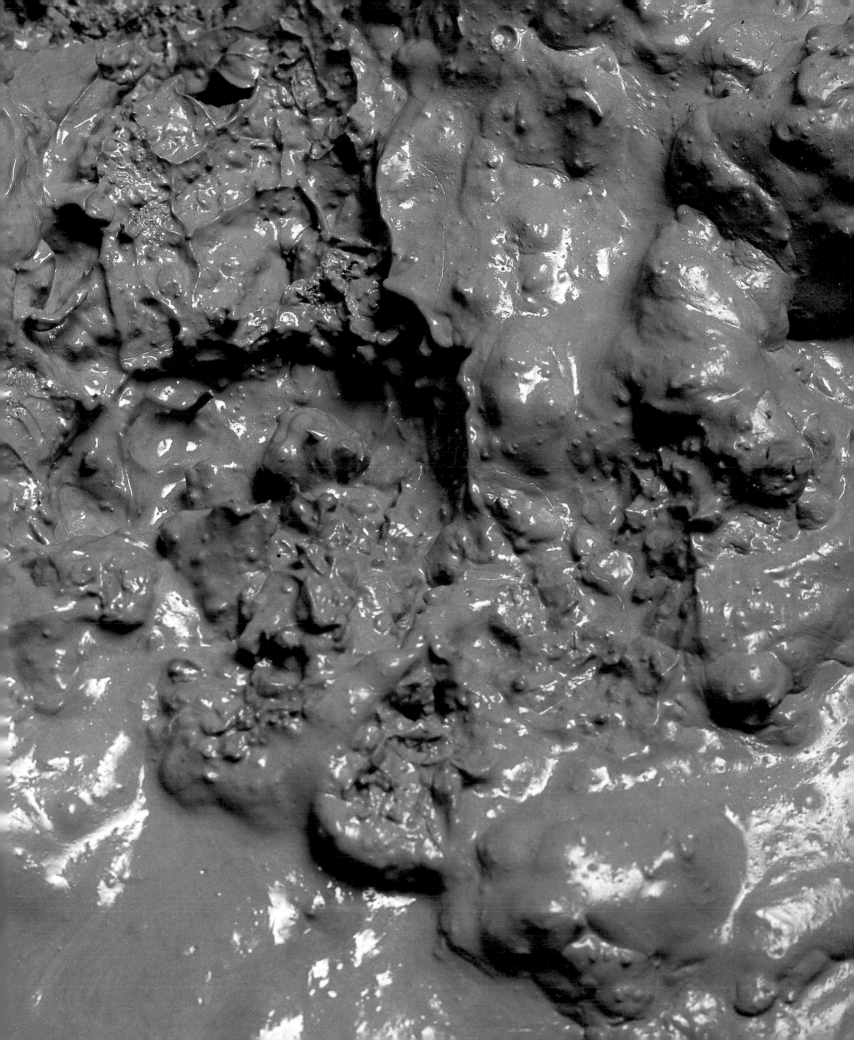

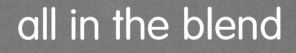

For potters, those various types can be used creatively to put together blends of clays, called 'bodies', which suit the particular needs of their ware. To make flowerpots, we need a clay that responds well to being pushed about. So it must be 'open' and not too dense, or it will require too much strength simply to work it. It must be plastic – that is good at bending without cracking – and reasonably smooth, or it will simply tear and split apart as it spins around. It must also be tough when it is dry for, if it's too sandy, it will be liable to collapse when being stacked in the kiln.

Today, we are digging the main ingredient of the body we use at Whichford; the sandy-coloured, silty top seams of our local pit, laid down on the edge of a local sea a mere 25 million years ago. On its own, it is a rather violent orange colour once fired, prone to cracking when drying out and warping out of shape in the heat of the kiln.

For that reason, we add a measure of a Staffordshire fireclay. This clay is of a very even temperament and it is pale, which balances the colour. It dries out fast which is useful, but is rather difficult to work because it's too short – not elastic enough – and so we have to add a third ingredient, a Thames Valley clay. This adds malleability and great strength. On its own though, it is extremely water-retentive and would be impossibly difficult to dry out. Together, however, these three clays combine to make a smooth, easily shaped clay that is reasonably docile while drying out and stands up to the testing fires of the kiln.

Far left: The fired Whichford body, showing the characteristics of a classic low-fired terracotta – coarse grained, slightly porous and a warm orange colour. This pot is decorated with the Whichford roulette.

Centre and left: The three different raw clays used at Whichford, each shown as dug (centre) and when mixed with water to make slip (left). Colour at this stage, when the clays are still just mud, bears no relation to fired colour; the top and bottom (local clay and Thames Valley clay) would end up bright orange, while the middle clay (Staffordshire fireclay), would be a pale pink.

frostproofing clay

Above: Flowerpot clay must be frostproof, so that it can be used outside in all weathers. This is achieved from a combination of careful sourcing, good preparation and a hot enough firing in the kiln.

It is ten o'clock by the time I return, following the first full lorry through the country lanes. The villages lie below us in the vales, held in place amongst the fields of yellow stubble by a matrix of green hedgelines. Eventually we come to a wide top, on the last eastward slopes of the Cotswolds.

It is here, on a disused airfield, that we store our freshly dug clay outside to weather. Whichford clay has to be frostproof, as we give a ten-year guarantee against frost damage. So, I inspect the lines of weathering clay with a keen eye as the first of this year's loads arrives, making sure that it is the right colour and consistency.

This batch will not be made into pots for another two years or so. As long ago as the 16th century in England there were laws regarding the ageing of clay that was to be used outdoors – for example for roof tiles, strict regulations were thought necessary to ensure that the wares were frostproof.

For the same reasons, we weather our clay, turning it regularly. I am often asked what it is that makes a clay frostproof, and good clay preparation is an important part of the answer. After much reading and research (we recently funded a PhD student on the topic), the subject still remains, as with so much to do with clay, a slight mystery to me. Good preparation both in weathering and refining, sufficient firing temperature and, above all, a clay body whose nature allows the frost to expand within it are all-important. If the structure of the clay is too tightly knit, with no air gaps included in it, then it is quickly destroyed by frost action.

On my way home, I freewheel down the long hill to Whichford. The road falls steeply and straight between rows of old oaks, then furrows round two sharp bends under high banks overhung by ash which suddenly open out, showing the village pond and, beyond that, the green. I remember the first time I ever came to Whichford, two decades ago, later in the autumn than this. I was surprised and delighted to find this hidden village neatly placed just so on the bridge of land between two streams. It is like a perfectly positioned ornament in the garden of the landscape.

That long, low barn at the back that one can see behind the old houses, is the pottery. It, too, is connected to its locality by a network of hedges, tracks and gardens planted over the years, so that most do not now realise that it is, in fact, a new building, not the old barn that it pretends to be.

I bump up the track, past the chickens who share their patch with ten young walnut trees and the inevitable pile of old flowerpots marooned behind the hedge. The footpath from the car park dips under an arch of flowerpots (more about that later!), then an arch of hedge. Everyone who works in the pottery is sat around in the courtyard garden, just finishing their tea break in the morning sun.

clay refining

I follow Richard, who looks after and blends our clay, round to the clay pile. We discuss my early morning foray while standing next to our three different raw clays, each with its own special nature, but all lumpy and quite unusable until refined.

At Wrecclesham, we had a simple system of refining. Shovel clay into a pit six feet by four feet and eighteen inches deep, add some water (the tricky bit is to get the amount right), cover with sand and trample down. Leave for a week and then dig out through a pugmill.

But I get ahead of myself. Why the sand? Think of those cracks in a summer field of clay ground: the bane of a potter's life is the cracks that appear as the clay dries, shrinks, and so pulls apart. The only cure, apart from mollycoddling and slow-drying, is to add a 'temper' or filler to the body which opens it up and reduces the amount of shrinkage. The easiest filler is sand and, at Wrecclesham, it was cannily added so it also stopped your boots sticking to the clay. More sophisticated bodies use grog – ground-up, already-fired pots or clay – and this is what we use at Whichford.

Filtering out lime

Alas, not everything in raw clay is welcomed by potters. As an apprentice at Wrecclesham, I had to spend many hours sifting the raw, dry clay by hand, picking out 'race', as we called fragments of stone. Anything to do with lime is particularly disastrous. Dormant throughout the making process, the high temperatures of kilning turn any fragment of limestone into quicklime. When put outside in the garden, this combines with water and, over some days, expands six times with unstoppable force, blowing fragments off the finished pots – not a welcome result.

There is only one sure way to to avoid this, laborious though it is. Add a lot of water to your clay and mix it thoroughly and you will get a slop the consistency of double cream, known as a slip. This can then be passed through a sieve removing all unwanted impurities.

The blunger

This is what we do at Whichford. Richard's first job, indeed the first in the whole process of pot making, is to shovel up the correct proportion of our three clays and add some water into a 400-gallon mixing tank, called a blunger. There, it is slopped and battered about until it forms a thick slip. Our blunger is an ancient machine, with fine cast-iron panels tastefully decorated in the late Victorian style. It was made by one of the original great engineering firms of the Industrial Revolution, Wm. Boulton & Co.

The clay room is not for the nervous. The blunger is just the first in an eclectic grouping of venerable machines, most of which weigh several tons, and there is much juddering, whining and whirring emanating from dark, clay-bespattered corners. A few over-inquisitive moves, a slither or two, and you could end up swimming in a subterranean storage vat of cold, thick slip.

Before the Industrial Revolution gave us all this machinery, my blunger would have been a barrel, with a lad and a long stick. The slip would be run out through a sieve (which the lad would keep kicking and poking to keep it clear) into a long, brick-lined trough. Here the clay, protected from the rain, would dry out into 5cm (2in) thick, crusty slabs. Eventually it would be cut, rolled up and taken to the potters.

Today, we use the more modern system of a filter press to push enough water out of the slip to get back to a plastic clay. Slip is pumped into cloth-lined chambers under a continuous pressure that is high enough to force water through the cloth walls, leaving only clay inside. After a few hours of this, the chambers (held in place between cast-iron plates) can be opened. Then, out fall the slabs of clay, caught on trolleys whose drunken wheels tell of habitual overloading.

At this stage, the clay is still uneven and needs mixing before it can be used. Traditionally, this was done by wedging – a slab of clay is cut with a thin piece of wire, the two halves are wedged back together, then re-cut until all lumps disappear. Or the clay would be mixed on the floor, using bare feet, especially the heels. It would involve treading rhythmically in ever-expanding circles over the pile of lumpy clay, folding it back on itself, and then repeating several times until smooth.

The mechanical alternative is called a pugmill, a machine that works on the idea of an Archimedes screw to chop up and compress clay. These appeared in England with the Industrial Revolution. In the country potteries, they were powered by a horse or mule that would walk in endless circles to turn the screw. We have a number of pugmills. The first, I built when I started, using a piece of 43cm (17in) water main for its barrel. Our oldest one has a brass plate dated 1894 riveted proudly onto its rusty shoulder. But the biggest and newest to us is 6m (20ft) long, an enormous

cylinder laid along the floor with various bits sticking out of it. Perhaps because of its pale greeny-blue colour, it doubles in my imagination as a surreal submarine floating among the reefs of clay that surround it.

In all pugmills, clay thrown in one end is chopped and minced while being pushed along the tube by blades, coming out the other end a long, smooth, well-mixed sausage. It can be used immediately, but is best left to rest for a few weeks (Chinese potters using porcelain, a notoriously unplastic body, would lay down clay for their grandchildren to use, to improve its workability).

This is also the stage at which the temper or filler is added to the clay to open out the body. As I said earlier, we use grog, which is a finely ground already-fired clay, and add about 6 per cent by weight – a handful to each good-sized slab. This opens out the clay structure and allows big pots to dry evenly and resist thermal shock better in the kiln. In addition, a pinch of grog acts like thousands of tiny ball bearings inside the clay, making it more amenable to being pushed into shape by the struggling potter!

At the moment, the mixed colour of our raw clay is light brown, but I have also used bodies of a deep red and a dark grey. Sometimes it is changed because a seam runs out, sometimes after new tests beckon one towards the potters' Holy Grail of the perfect, all-forgiving clay. But whatever the colour and character during the making, Whichford clay always displays key properties once out of the kilns. It must be frostproof; it must be orange; and it must be sufficiently porous.

In my experience, this porosity is important because it allows the pots to acquire a beautiful patina with age; and it also contributes to healthy root growth. But there is an historical argument about this that raged with surprising acrimony through the newborn gardening weeklies during the latter part of the 19th century.

Facing page: Finishing the many processes of refining, the pugmill chops, mixes and finally compresses the clay into a useable state.
Above: Cut slabs of clay await their turn to be sent up to the makers.

Above: Glazed flowerpots offer a great range of colours to the gardener, though opinions have always differed as to whether they are as good for root growth as plain terracotta.

It all started with a long, provocative letter to the *Gardener's Chronicle* in 1841 by Mr Forsyth, the Earl of Shrewsbury's gardener at Alton Towers, proposing the use of glazed flowerpots. In other words, he was arguing the merits of non-porous containers over the traditional water-permeable unglazed earthenware. The reaction among the gardening fraternity was initially unanimous. They condemned the plan as a bad one, citing the general welfare of plants, good drainage and a ready supply of air to the roots as the main benefits of porous pots.

In 1850, George W Johnson, editor of the rival *The Cottage Gardener*, hedged his bets, stating that 'gardeners are very far from unanimous in their opinion as to the material of which [flowerpots]

are made most beneficially'. His guarded opinion was that 'we verily believe, that almost every material of which a flowerpot can be made has some especial merit and disadvantage.'

Seven years later, however, he had made up his mind. 'It was formerly considered important to have [flower] pots made of a material as porous as possible; but a more miserable delusion never was handed down untested from one generation to another. Stoneware and Chinaware are infinitely preferable, for they keep the soil more uniformly moist and warm.' It is an opinion still in print, unchanged long after his death, in the 1917 edition of *The Cottage Gardener's Dictionary*.

The argument rumbled on throughout the Victorian era and, indeed, has never been resolved. For myself, I have noticed that porous clay seems to protect better against extremes, either of heat, cold or waterlogging. Also, if plants get overlooked and dry out, I find that they have a longer chance of survival in clays.

Seeing red

A subject nearly as hotly debated in the annals of Victorian gardening as that of porosity was the colour of flowerpots. *The Cottage Gardener* once again led the crusade with a Mr R Fish, in the January 1851 issue, (perhaps suffering from seasonal peevishness): 'I would banish the common red pot altogether from the windows of those who made any pretensions to refined taste, and where means allowed them that gratification. Amateurs here must take no lesson from gardeners.'

The opposing view is nicely summed up in an anonymous letter to the rival *Gardener's Chronicle* in 1857: 'Your correspondent is quite right as to the curious anomaly that those who are so capable of appreciating beauty in one particular are totally insensible in another. Red being the complementary colour to green, which after all is the prevailing colour in plants even in flower, is the fittest for pots, the only variation from which allowable is a brownish red for very light bright flowers, and a yellowish red for darker.' And the debates echo on across the years, with gentlemen amateurs and head gardeners on both sides appealing to the new certainties of scientific fact.

Red, or rather orange, is a good foil in the garden. A new clay pot is bright in colour, but it does not take much time before it begins to tone down and acquire that beautiful patina of old terracotta. This is partly achieved by the salts that are leached out of the compost, and partly by algae, which soon blends a flowerpot into its surroundings, leaving gentle hints of orange to support the greens around.

Modern taste will, however, also allow you to experiment with a wider range of colours without the risk of censure. At Whichford we have developed a less traditional range of colour coatings which we fire onto the pots, giving various pale ochres and an ash blue that cries out to be coupled with glaucous foliage and white, blue or yellow flowers.

Below: The colour of most fired clay ranges from pale cream, through pink, to orange. All these are colours which enhance green, as shown in these fine 19th-century prints.

But, to return to the practicalities. Clay making is physically tough, with many hours a week lugging clay from one pile to another. It also carries with it an unenviable price, which I have witnessed in every traditional pottery I have visited – indeed it is a standard joke. The claymen are forever being shouted at by the potters if the clay is either too soft, or too hard, or too lumpy, or too short or…

At Whichford, Richard and Brian have worked hard over the years to keep a steady flow of five tons of clay a week delivered to the potters, and they usually succeed. But a material as ancient and mysterious as clay is not easy to control. Sometimes it seems to be the temperature of the clay pile, or was one of the clays a little paler this week? As so often with clay (or gardening), we end up relying most on our intuitive understanding and, in the final reckoning, this is often more accurate than all the scientific records of temperatures, densities, shrinkages and so on that we also keep.

I seem to be building a picture of us potters as a temperamental bunch. To be a good maker, especially a thrower, there needs to be a certain tension about the work which, when thwarted, can snap and flare. How could you transform inert mud into the spinning form of your imagination without that spark? And if the clay is too soft to hold the shape, what frustration is felt as one's creation sags and buckles between one's hands. Or if it is too hard, how one cries out in anger as the pot whirls round on the wheel, stiff and unrelenting, refusing to co-operate. It is well if the claymen have broad backs to bear the cussing for having sent up such pre-prepared disasters!

To avoid these scenes, Richard and Brian have learnt to concoct the best blend from the many different stacks in the clay room. All are aged for at least three weeks after processing, a time which allows the clay to settle down and become noticeably more workable. Today, the clay is perfect, smooth, plastic and co-operative. Which is just as well, for this second half of the morning, I have the task of originating a new design.

My design aesthetic

I am often asked where our new designs at Whichford come from. I can give the textbook answer – all about tradition and influences – but ultimately it is intuitive. Indeed, it is very like the act of writing itself, where the thread of an idea will weave you in and out of your experiences to create something new, unexpected, yet something that you still recognise.

My hope is that, if I am well grounded in my own European tradition and conversant with its particular cultural attributes and preferences, then any new design I undertake will have that feeling of familiarity, even if it is, in fact, new. This is the obverse of art that seeks to break the mould and which uses shock to stimulate discussion. At Whichford, our political statement is enshrined in how we work – locally and in community, and with a sense of stewardship for our tradition. We work with the hope of passing it on so that it will be understood by the next generation, who will then update and develop it in their turn.

Standard sizing

When it comes to flowerpots, the English potters and gardeners of the 19th century co-operated to produce a range of pots that would suit all eventualities of plant needs, displaying a happy marriage between the aesthetically pleasing and the practical. In their simple way, these pots still provide a firm training in the basic relationships of form.

The standard English flowerpot has equal height and width at 15cm (6in). As they grow, larger pots need to diminish in relative height in order to keep these visually satisfying proportions. Thus, a 45cm (18in) wide pot at only 35cm (14in) in height looks exactly the same as the 15cm (6in) pot.

It was a point often not understood. Various 19th-century attempts, including by the Royal Horticultural Society, to completely standardise relative sizes met with little success, and there was much local variation. I take the Hampshire, Wrecclesham system as my yardstick, but also incorporate elements from elsewhere. Our standards have narrow bases, but we also make kitchen garden pots, broad in the base and so nearly vertical-sided, which is a much older variant.

The range of pots

Shallower than standards are alpine pans, or half pots, which are two-thirds of the height of standards, while seedpans, or 'storepots' are shallower still, being only one-third of standard height. As the names of these pots imply, their design is a compost-saving device. Why plant shallow-rooted seedlings in deep compost? It is also easier to simulate rocky mountain or semi-arid conditions in shallower pots. Deep-rooted plants, on the other hand, or many bulbs such as hyacinths, prefer longtoms, which add an extra third to standard height.

One of the great plant hunters of the 19th century, Sir Joseph Banks, is credited with inventing the hanging orchid pot to allow the hothouse cultivation of epiphytic orchids. An ordinary plant pot was given three small holes under its rim to hold hanging chains. Its sides were then perforated with 1cm (½in) holes in order to allow air to reach the orchid's roots; a classic design that we still make today.

Rhubarb forcers were also a 19th-century invention. In 1815, the chance burial of a rhubarb patch at the Chelsea Physic Garden led to the discovery of blanched rhubarb stems. Thomas Andrew Knight and the head gardener at his Edmonton estate went on to devise a long clay pot to 'force' the crop by denying it light, giving the delicate pink stems we know today. Seakale, and even chicory, forcers soon followed. These were traditionally produced alongside the crocks used in country food production – breadcrocks, pans, pancheons, salting troughs and dishes and the crockery used in farmhouse kitchens – so the whole range of work holds the same aesthetic.

Simple, utilitarian pots made especially for flowers first appeared in England in the late 17th century, answering the needs of the first large nurseries as they responded to the new middle-class craze for gardening. Before this time, pots used for flowers were multi-purpose and had often already been used for something else – a mixing bowl that was cracked or a posset jug that had lost its handle. There were also a few special items decorated in the style of the day, designed to hold a rare, beautiful or medicinal plant.

The use of orange trees by the Italians in Renaissance gardens spawned a line of very large flowerpots. This started a vogue for decorative garden urns in stone or terracotta that survived the 18th-century Landscape Movement, when most other garden clutter was cleared away. This is another important source of inspiration.

Below: At the heart of our range are utilitarian designs from the 19th century (the forcers to the left, seedpans in the centre and plain pots to the right). Other grander designs (the urn on the left is in late 17th-century style, the baskets and Italianate pots from later) mix with modern forms such as the elliptical pot (centre).

Today, though, I will be designing a hybrid: I need a pot to hold the lilies which we will offer our customers by mail order in the winter. It will therefore need to be robust so as to withstand the journey, relatively easy to make to keep the cost down and, most important of all, deep enough for the lilies. Practicality prescribes me a tall, thin shape, to which I must now add suitable decorative flair.

I usually think designs out on paper first, then develop them using 14lb balls of clay which, coincidentally, gives a good-sized pot for posting. My design remit is straightforward: I take a plain longtom shape which gives sufficient depth for the lilies, and embellish it. I do this first on the wheel by forming fancy rims or foot rings as the pot spins, then by adding a simple three-dimensional decoration on the wall of the pot. This time, I am going to try adapting a bold 19th-century print of a lily; a single flower which I have drawn and photocopied at various different sizes.

Once I have thrown a few trial pots, I try out the photocopies on the various pots, experimenting with different sizes and positions. I ask anyone passing for their opinions in the hope that they will warn me off the least successful ideas. This approach can be risky as I am quite shy and unsure about new designs. Early drafts are usually far from perfect, and will be modified several times before they begin to work. Negative reaction early on can discourage a good line of thought. On the other hand, it can be very exciting involving the team, each with their own skill. Today, there is general agreement about which is the best image and size, but much shifting around of it. We cannot agree if the flower should point up or hang down. We even try it sideways. In the end, I, or was it Rachel, hung the flower from just under the rim and suddenly it worked. Like many good ideas at the pottery, we could not remember whose idea it was, and it is then that I get an extra thrill of satisfaction; joint ownership of creativity is one of the best fruits of good teamwork.

Above: Low-relief decoration shows up well on flowerpots while leaving the shape of the pot relatively unaltered. An original is meticulously carved into clay (a job I like doing in comfort at the kitchen table) and from this a plaster mould is taken, which is then used to produce copies.

Facing page: The same crest embossed from the mould onto a very large pot, part of a special commission for Mr & Mrs Stephen Clark's garden at Seend Manor in Wiltshire, where a row of pots float magnificently on a clipped sea of low box hedging. Compared to the original, a few details are smudged, but it is still a good working copy.

I was given my first pot plant by my aunt when I was eight, a *Begonia* x *argenteoguttata*, and its many-times great-grandchild, propagated by cuttings, is still in my garden. When I grew up and had my own garden, I copied my mother and grew old-fashioned geraniums in pots – they are here too, as are the ferns and hostas I soon developed a taste for, enjoying the north-facing shade of an angle in the house. Finally, multi-species plantings, of the sort I have been taught and encouraged to use since showing at the Chelsea Flower Show, are ranged under and along the retaining wall that holds back the garden as it rises away from the house.

In other words, this private corner shows the rather eclectic style of my family, an informal higgledy-piggledy arrangement of flowers, pots and oddments. They tend to form groups, the different shapes in conversation with each other. Large pots stand high-shouldered at the back and the smallest pots huddle under their skirts, like so many children, held by their mother's hand in some old photograph.

The great advantage is that it can be changed or added to, according to whim, depending on what is looking good, or the season. New pots or plants can find a home amongst old favourites – and it all feels relaxed, right for a well-used family space.

Not that I am advocating a complete free-for-all. This mêlée is held firmly in place by the surrounding walls and flags, the hard landscaping. Nature is rampantly creative and gardening is the art of channelling that energy to achieve some new version and vision of paradise. The structure of a garden underpins the whole endeavour, and is what marks out all successful works of art, not least a garden. Learning first to perceive it in the work of others and then to create one's own version as experience grows, is one of the joys of becoming a true gardener.

Facing page: A flowerpot arch marks the entrance to the Pottery. Round its base we use an eclectic collection of jars and pots. The box shapes will stay there all year, but the others will be replaced or replanted every season.

Above: A single pot by Devon potter Svend Bayer acts as a focal point in the garden of another potter and sculptor, Gordon Cooke.

A good example of this interplay between structure and freedom can be seen at the main entrance to the pottery itself. Leaving your car in the car park, you approach the main building and the garden in front of it on foot through an arched gap in a tall hawthorn hedge. But before you enter the garden you will pass under another arch, no green hedge, but rather two crazy corkscrews of flowerpots meeting overhead in a spray of tiny pots.

This piece was thought up one year when casting around for ideas for the Chelsea Flower Show. We had often done snakes of pots on the ground – why not in the air? The fantasy took off and we ended up with double helixes of small 7.5cm (3in) pots held in the air by steel rods: a model of the structure of DNA, flowerpots as the very stuff of life itself!

The arch always raises a smile and it certainly gives a structural start to the garden at the pottery. It is linked to the next hedge arch by evenly spaced pairs of pots flanking the path, usually planted with clipped box balls – all very formal.

This hard landscaping is softened, however, by boisterous plantings around the legs of the flowerpot arch. The formal structure of path, arch and box balls provides a foil for the exuberance of the opening groups of pots, which indeed are chosen fairly randomly.

These plantings are looked after by Issy. It is a mark of her skill that some of our summer plantings are still looking at their riotous best well into the autumn. Because she has been deadheading regularly all summer, the half-hardy plants that are our staples are still full of flower. One large pot is almost invisible beneath its skirts of yellow *Bidens ferulifolia* and pink verbenas. The soft silver *Helichrysum petiolare* is a thick block of grey foliage. It is a strong grower and,

left to its own devices, would by now have engulfed half the pot or become straggly and thin. When deadheading the flowering plants, Issy will have been pinching out the tips to encourage sideways, bushy growth. In plants where this is not done, or is too laborious, as with the trailing lobelias that are past their best, now is the time to be ruthless and clear away.

This can leave some rather alarming gaps, with bare earth and the underside of surrounding plants showing woody stems and dead underfoliage. For just this eventuality, Issy has brought out a few small pots, perhaps the bright orange and maroon of tagetes or, elsewhere, the more tolerant glaucous rosettes of echeverias.

Below: In his garden in Oxfordshire, Andrew Lawson uses just a hint of hard landscaping – a line of cobbles in gravel – to hold together a square of small pots, and thus gives form to his sprawling groups of autumn colour.

Facing page: A frescoed loggia at Whichford makes a striking background for this planting of a fastigiate berberis, a zonal pelargonium and purple-leaved heucheras. It will continue to flourish until a hard frost takes out the pelargonium.

Above: An antique Devon salting trough underpins a riot of autumn colour, led by the *Dahlia* 'Bishop of Llandaff'. The morning glory has grown all summer until it now reaches the first-floor windows.
Facing page: A summer planting given new bones for the autumn – badger skulls and a dressing of gravel fill the gaps left by withered summer lobelias.

autumn plantings

I love the tattered glory of a September garden. I have planted a pair of borders in the round garden near the house to be at their best in this season, with as many bright, vibrant colours as I can manage. While many plants seem to become more mellow in colour during the autumn, these borders lift the spirits with the startling yellow of rudbeckias setting off the magenta *Phlox paniculata* and the purples and mauves of a selection of asters. A few clumps of late-flowering monkshood bring darker blues and, at the back, *Eupatorium purpureum* (Joe Pye weed) is still holding up large clusters of dusty pink flowers. I do not remember all of the variety names of these perennials but, as long as they do their job every year, who cares?

In the middle of each border are two enormous flowerpots, covered with exuberant decoration. Their plantings are still providing plenty of colour and will do so until the first hard frost. There's dark orange *Abutilon megapotamicum*, yellow argyranthemums and red pelargoniums. The red of the pelargoniums is picked up by a clear red dahlia, a pot of which I have squeezed in amongst the perennials. It is still flowering madly.

Delightful dahlias

Although we are still relying on the show that we are coaxing from our main summer plantings, there are also a few choice autumn pots which can now be pulled out into prominence. Our latest favourites are dahlias, which offer plenty of scope for the hottest colours. *D.* 'Bishop of Llandaff' is a clear red single with a yellow eye. Its bronze, spiky leaves look good on their own as they grow throughout the summer, long before the flowers appear. We have planted some orange 'David Charles' with another late flowerer, *Canna* 'Wyoming', again bronze-leaved with orange flowers.

Chrysanthemums can add colour in the same way as dahlias, but there is something rather neat about having to keep an eye on the half-hardy dahlias. I find they are somehow less easy to forget, and therefore lost to frost, if kept out of the borders in pots. Indeed, I have taken to growing simple medium-sized pots full of dahlias and using them in my borders to fill autumn gaps with colour in much the same way as Issy uses her little pots by the arch to fill out the summer plantings.

There are also the autumn bulbs and corms, all of which thrive in pots with a minimum of care. We choose frost hardy varieties, so that they can be left out all the year. We use *Cyclamen hederifolium* both by itself and in miniature arrangements, choosing the plants with the strongest silver markings on dark leaves, and purply pink flowers. We plant up a little pan of naked ladies (*Colchicum*) in pink or white, and a big pan or shallow basket of glorious *Nerine bowdenii* 'Pink Triumph'. This is the one we will now bring right to the front of our display, underplanted with a few wisps of *Senecio cineraria* and smartened up with a layer of fresh gravel to cover the bare compost.

Autumn is a season of sudden changes. It starts with the fullness of late summer with half-hardy *Bidens ferulifolia* (top, second from left) billowing out from under the fronds of a Tasmanian tree fern, and ends with frost on the first plantings of winter (top, far right and bottom, second from left), which rely for their effect on the strong forms of box or mahonia. In between are autumn's own moments of glory – the blaze of *Dahlia* 'Red Riding Hood' (bottom, left), kniphofia and species fuchsias at their best (bottom, far right) and the tiny gems of cyclamen among turning leaves (top left and top, second from right).

Successful succulents

Another group of plants that come into their own in the autumn are succulents. Ever since I started growing in pots, I have enjoyed using the many varieties of houseleeks. Not for nothing are they known as sempervivum, or 'everliving'. Their ability to survive anywhere as long as there is enough light and not too much water makes them an ideal candidate for flowerpots, especially for those that live a long way from a tap. They look their best at this time of year, when the older mother rosettes are surrounded by their silently jostling children. Sempervivums can survive harsh winters, and I have often seen them high up in the Southern Alps.

More care is needed with my other favourite succulent, echeveria, which must be overwintered in a cool greenhouse, with the temperature kept above freezing. Last year, I was given a tiny handful of strange succulents by a Japanese friend. We decided to treat them as we do our echeverias, so Issy laid them out loose on the greenhouse bench. This seems to have been the right thing to do for, after a few days, they began to sprout tiny, white, hair-like roots.

We potted them up in a compost cut with some fine grit to aid drainage, then treated them as any other plant, except for trying to avoid watering the middle of their crowns. We did lose one from the grey mould of botrytis. In the spring, we put the little plants outside in their final pots, dressed with gravel. All summer they swelled and grew until now, in autumn, their outlandish shapes have filled the pots – fleshy, crimped cabbages sprinkled with pink, or pagodas of crazily stacked red prisms.

Below: Gordon Cooke, a potter based in Manchester, makes striking pots based on natural forms. The shape here is abstracted from an opening flower and a tiny landscape of sedums flourishes in its protection.

Facing page: Like a fossil found by chance on a beach, this ammonite curls protectively around a single aloe aristata and a few carefully placed pebbles in a thoroughly modern setting.

The fleshy rosettes of succulents are particularly suited to growing in pots, which can easily be made to mimic their natural, semi-arid habitat. These ones shown here come from a wide range of genera including the deepest purple of *Aeonium*, the blue-grey of *Echeveria*, the tiny leaves of *Sedum* and *Sempervivum*. The red spikes and strangely formed green succulents (left of caption) came from Japan and are a mystery to us. With the exception of the house leeks (sempervivums), all will need the protection of a cold greenhouse before the first frost. Many of the species are at their best in autumn, putting out their spikes of flowers as the tips of their leaves tinge pink or red. Aeoniums and echeverias will become tall plants on long stems over the years, with the stalk which supports their rosettes growing about two centimetres (an inch) a year.

stem-tip cuttings

After lunch, I decide that my design work can wait and I shall spend a happy couple of hours taking cuttings. Like any season, much of the work in autumn is preparing for next season or next year (which is what makes gardening so enthralling, giving you that never-ending prospect of something new).

Our displays are all ten times the size they were when planted out, and the bulk of the growth is only half-hardy. I have room for a few specimens in the greenhouse, but most plants will be left flowering until they die in the first frosts. I have to decide now which species I will keep going myself over winter with cuttings, and which I shall restock next year with new plants.

I arm myself with a pair of secateurs and a few clear plastic bags in a basket and begin a tour of our plantings. I look for the healthiest plants – avoiding anything that is either straggly or yellowing – and search out strong non-flowering shoots, cutting them at least 7.5cm (3in) long for most plants. I immediately place each species into its own plastic bag. If you are very organised (or forgetful), you can add a copy of the plant's name label.

I try not to be over-ambitious at this stage – there is a lot more work to do – but collecting cutting material is one of these jobs that, once started, leads you on! Better, after half a dozen plants, to rush to the table in the greenhouse and transform your bunches of greenery into cuttings proper. Although, if you close the plastic bag well, the material will keep overnight in the fridge before processing.

The principle of stem-tip cuttings is very simple. Strip the stem of leaves with a sharp scalpel or pair of scissors, leaving only the tip and its two leaves. Push the cuttings into a pot of compost, in a hole made with an old pencil, and water well.

We do not bother with rooting hormone powder or fungicide, but do increase the drainage of the compost by adding at least one part of perlite to three of compost. The great enemy of cuttings is botrytis mould, so the cuttings are checked frequently. All susceptible material, such as damaged leaves or incipient flowers, are removed.

Compost and propagation

The cardinal rule for successful cuttings is to keep the compost damp until the new plant has developed root – which will only take a few weeks for most half-hardy material. In addition, gentle heat encourages growth. You can buy a ready-made propagator, complete with underfloor heating unit and ventilated clear cover, and these certainly work well.

Alternatively, individual pots of cuttings can be covered by plastic bags held in place by a rubber band (careful the leaves don't touch the plastic or they will rot). Or use half an upended plastic bottle. These systems not only help prevent the compost drying out, but also keep the leaves moist while they await fresh supplies of water from the new root system. Kitchen window-sills are an ideal place for cuttings – they are warm and you can keep an eye on them.

At Whichford, we take a lot of cuttings, so we have built ourselves a large propagator. I have nailed 15cm (6in) high sides to the edge of an old trestle table and snaked into that a low-watt heating cable buried in 7.5cm (3in) of old potting compost. A simple wooden frame holds up a plastic tent over the whole contraption, and there is a thermostat supplied with the cable that controls the temperature. I set it at 15°C (59°F) for cuttings, as a higher temperature can encourage the formation of a thick callous at the base of the cutting, which can hinder root growth.

We use clay pots for our cuttings, placing about a dozen shoots around the edge of a 15cm (6in) half pot, so that the terracotta will draw moisture towards the cuttings. Once the cuttings have struck roots, they will need to be gently separated and planted individually into 7.5cm (3in) pots. In a heated greenhouse like ours, they need to be potted on by late winter into 10cm (4in) pots. So, do not be over-enthusiastic with the number of cuttings. If you are short of some species, like us you can take cuttings off your cuttings in mid-winter!

These stem-tip cuttings use semi-ripe material rather than more mature hardwood. The latter take much longer to root, and are best done in a cold frame or sheltered patch of open ground.

Below: The charming flowers of *Semiaquilegia ecalcarata* set copious amounts of seed which we collect for later planting.

There are also some plants that we regularly use, such as clematis that we propagate from leaf-bud cuttings taken in mid-summer. We also take stem cuttings in summer from *Tricyrtis formosana* (toad lily) and *Lobelia cardinalis*. Both are good late-summer and early-autumn flowerers.

Cuttings are a good way of cheaply producing the large numbers of good-sized plants that we need all at once at the end of spring. We also grow large amounts of material from seed that we harvest as it becomes ripe from July onwards. By now we have already collected and sown seed from the best aquilegias and the pretty, purple *Semiaquilegia ecalcarata*. Before they ripened, we marked the heads with a strand of red wool and returned just before the dry pods split to spill out their seed, and put them in paper bags pilfered from the sales desk. Last week we collected a good dark red hollyhock, a white *Cleome spinosa* and a double *Papaver somniferum*, snipping off seed-heads and labelling them clearly as we went.

Today, I noticed the strange, pendulous fruits that hang from the cream-flowered annual climber, *Cobaea scandens*, were beginning to split and reveal their huge seeds, so I took some of those. I also remembered that a friend requested some seeds of the magenta perennial sweet pea in the round garden and somebody else had asked for *Thalictrum aquilegiifolium*; I do not normally bother to save that one, but allow it to seed itself (the same goes for *Nigella damascena*). Ripe seed-heads of *Lychnis coronaria*, another favourite, I shake straight over the borders – they seem happier to germinate like this rather than be pampered in a seed tray.

Once the seed is collected, we store the paper bags in the greenhouse where they will be kept dry. Except for the earliest summer seeds, which need sowing as soon as they are ripe, we wait to sow seed until early spring when there is more light and heating is more economical. Our cuttings will survive as long as we

Above: If you have a greenhouse, it is worth choosing a few favourite half-hardy specimens to grow on over winter, keeping other species going from cuttings only. This scarlet *Pelargonium* 'Paul Cramphorn' is in its fourth year.

keep the greenhouse frost-free, whereas seedlings are more vulnerable to fungal disease in cool conditions and low light levels.

For new species, we will often buy in strips of plugs filled with tiny, freshly germinated plants and grow them on, but it is more fun to try to keep existing strains going yourself. There is a particular satisfaction in looking at a complicated planting and realising that every plant has been nurtured in your own greenhouse.

Preparing for winter

As I go around collecting my cutting material, I also try to make a mental note of the few half-hardy specimens I want to lift and keep protected over the winter (it helps to leave a bamboo sticking out from them to remind you). These will need to be excavated out of their present home just before the first frost. I decide on some three-year-old *Felicia amelloides*, a nicely shaped argyranthemum,

and I cannot bear to lose those enormous old-fashioned 'Paul Cramphorn' pelargoniums.

Once they are lifted, they will all be cut back and have their rootball banged about to loosen the now-spent old compost. A certain amount of loose roots will be pulled off (root pruning), and then the plant will be put into a holding pot with new compost around the ball for the winter and kept in the greenhouse out of the frost.

I also have a good stock of hardy plants that will need similar sort of treatment, certainly to their rootballs. This job can be left until after the first frosts, but is best done before the onset of real winter. I am thinking in particular of the many clipped box shapes that we have, and which are going to be so important in giving winter structure. But the same applies to our myrtles (some variegated), phormiums and ferns if they start to look tired.

Box will soon let you know if its roots have not got enough new compost by a tell-tale bronzing of the leaves. With annual attention to the rootball and some foliar feeding through the growing season, a specimen box can be maintained in the same-sized pot for many years in good condition. In essence, what you have is an overgrown bonsai.

Other shrubs we use, such as the myrtles, pittosporum, buddleia, *Lonicera* x *purpusii*, or *Hamamelis mollis* do not respond so kindly to root pruning. You are left with the choice of either regularly increasing the size of pot used, or enjoying a year or two's use in flowerpots before liberating the shrubs to open sites in the garden.

I have been surprised at how well some shrubs have survived for many years in pots, for instance *Elaeagnus pungens* 'Maculata', hollies and hawthorn. They need little more than a top-dressing in the spring, where an inch or two of old, worn-out compost is scraped off the surface and replaced with fresh.

There is always much discussion about what ingredients make for the best potting compost. As with clay bodies for potters, potting composts are made up of all concoctions, each with their own particular uses.

The first priority in any compost is that it must be free-draining, otherwise the rootball will become waterlogged and the plant will literally suffocate. Air is just as important to roots as water, so the compost should not be too compacted. The old-fashioned way to ensure this is to use a peat-based compost, and I sometimes notice a bag or two of peat under our benches, although peat farming is ecologically unsustainable.

With reluctance, since peat is so good, we try to use coir or rotted bark instead, reserving a little peat for the special cases only. Coarse sand or grit added helps open out any compost, just as it does for clay. I use the John Innes family of loam-based composts less and less as they tend to compact down to a solid mass after a few weeks of heavy watering. The exception to this is with long-term plantings, where shrubs seem to enjoy the weight of John Innes No.3.

The second essential for compost is that it is full of nutrients, more than the plant needs, as many will be washed out with regular watering. The advent of slow-release fertilisers has revolutionised composts. In the past, John Innes had three strengths for the various stages of growth, as young plants would be gorged by the full-strength mix and older plants starved by the seedlings mix. Nowadays, one general compost can do everything, especially if you add a little blood, fish and bonemeal to the bottom layer of a big pot and are prepared to liquid feed foliage and add compost occasionally.

Left: Good potting compost must be open-textured enough to give air to the rootball, and full of nutrients to promote good leaf and flower growth.

My final job for the day is another that, once started, is hard to stop: choosing our spring bulbs. This weekend is our Bulb Bonanza show, and we have bought in a lorry-load of choice bulbs from Holland. They are now beautifully laid out in baskets on kilim-covered tables in the hastily cleared packing shed, awaiting the arrival of the eager public. I sneak in for a preview, and to choose with Issy what we will use ourselves in borders and pots next spring.

Bulbs are ideal for pot culture. In the borders they invariably get lost or inadvertently dug up at the wrong time, and there is always that uncertainty as to what to do with the half-wilted foliage – can I cut it back yet? In a pot, as long as you water well during dry spells, even in winter (very important, or you will stunt growth), the bulbs can be easily protected from slugs and snails. When over, the whole pot can be quietly moved to some shady corner to be allowed to die back gently in its own time.

In addition, pots provide a showcase for the bulbs as they develop, and their first firm sprouts are one of the great wonders of gardening. For years, we have gone one stage further at the pottery, and watched them grow even underground. We wanted to show the depths at which to plant different species, and also illustrate a multi-species bulb-only planting which would give flowers from mid-February through to mid-May. That way, we could disprove the familiar complaint that bulbs are 'no sooner out than over'. Someone suggested cutting a pot vertically in half and screwing a sheet of Perspex across the cut. Through the Perspex, every year you can see the different bulbs sprouting up to reach the surface – snowdrops first, then miniature iris, early tulips, narcissi, late tulips and, under all, a clump of crown imperials pushing up through a full 30cm (12in) of compost. Although this system does not strictly obey the maxim that you should plant a bulb to a depth two and a half times its height, it still works well, and enables us to

Facing page: Pots and bulbs are a natural combination. These amaryllis will produce enough huge trumpet flowers to brighten any winter table.

pack over 70 bulbs into a 52.5cm (21in) diameter flowerpot. We even overplant our pots with a covering of winter pansies and ivies. The spikes of bulbs push these aside as they break through the surface of the compost.

I leave the packing shed with two baskets creaking with the weight of the bulbs in them, and walk around the back of the pottery. The late sun is turning everything golden. I shall keep the bulbs dry and out of harm's way in the tool shed next to the vegetable garden. As I step into it, the smell of old sacks and dust mingles with that of the early apples which begin to fill the stacks of boxes. Some will be eaten, but most will be used by Adam to make cider.

As I go out, I stop for a moment and lean in the doorway. I am tired, but I am held there. When will I see such drowsy beauty again? I look down the valley to where the mist is beginning to rise. Tomorrow the rain and wind may begin.

Below: Autumn is the time of mists, fruit and cobwebs. Enjoy the warmth and sunshine while you can!

Many summer performers keep going well into the autumn if the first frosts are not too sharp or early. In fact some, such as many salvias and penstemons, are just reaching their prime in September. Here are some of the plants that come into their own from then until (if we are lucky) November. When creating autumn plantings we often combine them with the plants we have listed for winter and make sure they are underplanted with spring bulbs so as to carry the display as far as possible into the New Year.

Hardy Perennials
Kniphofia, eg 'Little Maid', 'Brimstone' **R; S; WD**
Lobelia cardinalis **S–PS; WD**
Sedum alboroseum 'Frosty Morn' **S; WD** (requires little soil)
Sedum 'Herbstfreude' **S; WD** (requires little soil)

Grasses (F)
Briza media **S–PS; WD**
Carex buchananii **S–PS; WD**
Hakonechloa macra 'Aureola' **S–PS; WD**
Hordeum jubatum **S; WD**
Imperata cylindrica 'Rubra' **R; S–PS**
Lagurus ovatus **S; WD**
Leymus arenarius
Pennisetum villosum **S; WD**

Bulbs
Colchicum speciosum. **S–PS; T; WD**
Crinum x *powellii* **R; S; WD**
Cyclamen hederifolium **R; WD**
Nerine bowdenii **S; T; WD**

Alpines/miniatures
Sempervivum arachnoideum **S; WD** (requires little soil)
S. tectorum – and many other sempervivums **S; WD** (requires little soil)

Deciduous shrubs
Acer palmatum **F; R; S–PS** (keep sheltered from winds)
Berberis thunbergii **Fc; S; WD**
Callicarpa bodinieri var. *giraldii* **S–PS; T; WD**
Cotoneaster horizontalis **S–PS** (produces autumn berries)
Pyracantha **S–PS** (produces autumn berries)

Bedding/tender
Canna – many, eg 'Durban', 'Wyoming'
Dahlia – many, eg 'Bishop of Llandaff', 'Summer Night' **S; WD**

Key
E: Prefers ericaceous compost
F: Interesting foliage
Fc: Foliage colours in autumn
P: Scented foliage or flowers
PS–Sh: Thrives in partial shade or shade
R: Likes a rich, fertile soil (add organic matter, such as leaf-mould)
S: Prefers a sunny site
S–PS: Will tolerate sun or partial shade
S–Sh Happy with either sun or shade
Sh: Thrives in a shady position
T: Talking-point/attention-grabber – people will ask you what that plant is!
WD: Requires a very well-drained soil that includes added grit or coarse sand.

Facing page, top left: English flowerpotters have always made a few glazed pieces as well as plain terracotta. This tulipière, based on a 17th-century design, holds a riot of autumn colour.
Top right: Simple pots full of the grass *Imperata cylindrica* 'Rubra' brighten up a flank of stone steps, each leaf reddening at the edges as autumn progresses.
Bottom: A sea-monster fountain head dances past small pots of echeverias and the first autumn pansies.

winter

Above: The Old Man of the Garden sits out the winter storms at Whichford.
Facing page: Plants must be frost hardy and have good structure. The variegated leaves of this *Euphorbia characias* ssp. *wulfenii* 'Emmer Green', give useful colour.

Even when you have lived with a landscape or a garden for many years, there are always new details to be chanced upon that surprise and delight in a sudden moment. But there is another kind of noticing – slower and deeper. In winter, when so much has been stripped away by the rains of autumn and the cold has withered all but the sturdiest of plants and foliage, you have the chance to see the shape and structure of hard elements. Gone is the finery and detail of the other seasons and revealed are the bones of landscape, garden and plants.

For those, like me, who enjoy discovering how things are made and held together, this is the time when you can come to know a place and how it really is underneath, without its bright costumes. Such revelation always sets me thinking and that, in turn, leads to new plans. I fantasise paths, flowerbeds or whole new rooms to add to the garden. Oddly, in so doing, I somehow come to see more clearly what is already there, even if few of the dreams are ever put into action.

This musing and dreaming suit winter well, especially when gazing into the log fire that burns every night in my old inglenook fireplace. Ideas uncurl like the first stirrings under bleak earth, the sharp rising spikes somehow sure of the coming spring that is nowhere yet to be seen. We seem to be wired directly into the ancient archetype of resurrection, inherent in the cycle of the seasons, and as long as we keep on cajoling and battling with Nature in our gardens, it will be forever so.

Nor is the business of making flowerpots immune to this cycle. Winter is our quiet time – who wants to think of choosing from a row of pots in the driving rain? It often requires a steady nerve and faith in what the turning wheel of the seasons will bring to carry on producing when the telephone is so quiet. But this is what we have to do; build up the stock that will eventually see us through the busy times that will come with spring and early summer.

Because winter is quiet, it is also the best time for training apprentices. Nowadays, most learning is paper based but, in the crafts, there is a more time-honoured way of acquiring knowledge. Apprentices work alongside and are helped by more experienced workers, or 'Masters'. This is a very practical way of learning and particularly suits the many skilled craftspeople who are dyslexic.

At Whichford, we have pioneered a return to an old-fashioned apprenticeship scheme, at the end of which students receive their NVQ, a nationally recognised vocational qualification. We have up to five apprentices at any one time.

The hardest thing about apprentices is that they leave. Luckily, we can often find jobs for them here, as someone moves away or just wants a change. In any working community change keeps the organisation healthy, like a good winter shuffle around in the herbaceous border. The new blood brings fresh ideas and questions habits that have become stuffy.

Below: Apprentices at Whichford train for between two and three years and have to learn about every aspect of making pots. Here Adam is changing a round pot which he has thrown on the wheel into an oval shape. Later, he will add lug handles at each end.

Above: A trolley load of big pots ready to be pushed on its rails into the kiln.

It's a cold, drizzling morning today, with a dim light struggling thinly and late through a pall of low cloud. I shiver quickly up the path to the pottery to seek out the various apprentices and see how they are faring.

Given the weather, my first port of call is the kiln room. Drawing, or unloading, the kilns is always a popular job first thing on a winter's day with the pots (too hot to touch without gloves) giving off a delicious heat. However, once the trolley is full of freshly baked pots, the doors are opened and you have to brave the elements to pull it to the stockyard. We have two main kilns in the heart of the pottery downstairs, which are both fired with gas. The waste heat that they generate keeps the workshops warm.

A slatted floor above the kilns allows the heat to pass through stacks of pots lined up for their vital final drying. It is a process

neglected at our peril, since any slightly damp pot put into the heat of the kilns will explode to smithereens as the trapped water from inside it boils, turns to steam and forces its way out. There are some laws of Nature that you simply have to obey!

Kiln loading

This simple rule observed, kiln loading is like some giant puzzle where the game is to fit as many differently shaped three-dimensional objects as possible into a given cube. It is a self-contained job, so ideal for apprentices to be given responsibility over as soon as possible – usually after a year's training. Since we fire about five kilns a week, they will have had plenty of practice during that year.

Kilns down the ages have been of many shapes and sizes, and have become increasingly sophisticated, but they all share some basic characteristics. A firebox that can burn copious amounts of fuel leads into a small room full of pots with a controlled exit for the flames once they have licked around the load. Because of the regular heating and cooling, the walls of kilns that were made from bricks were often several feet thick, shored up with buttresses and held together by thick iron straps. If a kiln worked, it would be passed down to future generations. I have seen kilns in Italy that date from the Renaissance still in use, and many 18th-century tile kilns still exist in France.

Our kilns at Whichford differ from these traditional kilns in that we have substituted gas for the usual wood – it involves a lot less work than manual stoking. Also, instead of large volumes of bricks for the structure, we have a steel cage lined with a highly efficient insulating ceramic fibre, a spin-off from the American Space programme. Apart from that, the design roughly follows that of a Chinese Sung Dynasty (960–1279 AD) down-draught kiln, where the flame is trapped inside the kiln for as long as possible, finally being sucked out by the draught from a chimney.

Filling it up

Today is the first time Rob is in charge of loading a kiln, so I am there to reassure and encourage him (and to make sure he does not make too many mistakes). The kiln trolley, about 1.5m (5ft) square, is pulled out and waits empty. Large pots are gently manoeuvred from the lift on to the trolley and stacked inside one another, four or five high, on props and shelves which allow air to pass all around each pot. Smaller pots used to fill up gaps are dropped or thrown through a hatch from upstairs to waiting hands below – a process that always alarms onlookers, but one enjoyed as a sport by those doing it.

Above: Joe checks that all is in order before he closes the kiln door. When it is next opened, in three days' time, the pots will have turned their characteristic orange colour.

It takes nearly two hours to load a kiln and, once filled, the trolley is shunted into the body of the kiln, the door clamped shut and the firing started. It will take between 18 and 32 hours to reach a temperature of over 1000°C (1832°F), when the pots will glow the colour of iridescent straw. Bigger pots need a longer, gentler firing to avoid cracking under the strain.

Cooling down then takes one or two days. If the pots are underfired, they will be too porous and not frostproof. If overfired, they will become a dark, hard red, shrink and eventually, at about 1100°C (2012°F), begin to melt into a bubbling mass of molten sticky rock.

Now at the end of his first year, Rob already knows a lot about what it takes to make pots. He will have spent time in the clayroom (today Richard is stamping and slapping his arms to keep warm; just as kilns in summer are a sweaty job, so clay in winter is often bitter cold). He has also learnt much about 'servicing'. This is what we call the many tasks involved in steering the pots through the drying process from the wheel to kiln, and keeping the workshop shipshape.

When I was a child, I was in great awe of the old gardener who tended the garden next door. He had been trained in late Victorian times and was now rather lame. So he usually welcomed the opportunity to sit down and regale me with stories of his distant youth. I was very young and I am left only with vague impressions from his stories. There were the endlessly swept gravel paths, days spent emptying wooden wheelbarrows filled with the prunings of more senior gardeners and late-night stokings in the crackling frost.

The apprentices at Whichford have to follow much the same path. Instead of gravel, this morning Rob will already have done his share of hoovering our wooden floors. Long-term exposure to clay dust can cause health problems and so we do this, our version of sweeping, at least once a day. For wheelbarrows, we substitute metal racks on wheels on to which freshly made pots are placed, and woe betide the new apprentice who fails to 'make space' for a thrower in full flow by not providing an empty trolley when needed. And twice a week there will be someone coming in late to check on the kilns.

Facing page: Basketware decoration is added to thrown pots which have first been allowed to stiffen slightly. Full drying, always completed upside down, takes an average of ten days.

drying pots

Between making and firing, the wet pots must be watched over meticulously. During this stage, the clay shrinks most, by about 9 per cent. If the drying out is too fast or too uneven, the pots will simply crack under the strain, most often in the base as a line or pair of lines growing like spokes off the central drainage hole. Avoiding this requires an intimate knowledge, not only of which pots can dry at what speed, but also where in the building they dry fast and where they dry slowly. In addition to this, a keen eye must be kept on the effect of the heat from the kilns and changes in the weather, both of which make an enormous difference to the speed of drying. In the summer, with windows and doors open for the breeze, drying is lightning fast, but now, with cold and rain, the building is clogged with damp pots. So we have our two dehumidifying rooms with mechanical drying facilities, as it is vital to keep the pots coming through.

As a pot is made, it is put high or low on the racks, according to its needs (high dries much faster). Then, after a day or three, once its rim has firmed up cnough to handle, it will be turned over on to a slatted rack and its base tidied up, or 'fettled'. After a few more days, or weeks if it is a big, slow-drying pot, it will have changed colour from a dark to a light reddish brown and look almost dry – dry enough to be past the danger of cracking. Rob and the other apprentices then move the pots above the kilns, where they are ranged in stacks for their final warming by the kilns' heat, before being dropped down through the hatches to the fire.

Left: The final drying of pots is on slatted floors above the kilns. Very large pots may take up to a month after making to get this far so as to avoid the cracks which can occur during the process – earthenware clay shrinks about 9 per cent between wet and dry state, and a further 3 per cent during firing.

decorating pots

Above: I begin throwing a pot on the wheel. It will be worked on and decorated over several days before it is finished.

Another job that all apprentices have to learn is that of decoration. To throw a pot, especially a large pot, it is best to use soft clay. If it is too hard, the struggle to centre the original lump on the wheel is too gruelling. However, the disadvantage of using soft clay is that it leaves the finished pot very fragile, wet and floppy to the touch. Little can be done to a pot in this state, so many are dried off slightly on the racks before being placed on a turntable, or banding wheel, and decorated.

This job is always done by women. On such a sensitive issue, I hesitate to advance theories as to why this should be so, but it has always been the case at Whichford, just as the throwing tends to be done by men. It is probably down to the simple mechanics of muscle power. Throwing needs large amounts of brute force, while decorating requires equally large amounts of gentler, but far more precise, stamina.

Today it is Liz who is the apprentice decorator, working under the eagle-eyed supervision of Rachel and Hilary. Of all the jobs in the pottery, this is the one that visitors always think looks the most fun, and I can see, or rather hear, why. As I climb the stairs from the kiln room, I hear a gale of laughter, led as always by Hilary. The three of them are sitting close together on a row of stools, each working on their own pot at a table in front of them, all set between two wheels and their throwers. It is hard to keep a secret here in such intimate surroundings and, while the odd tantrum has been known, gossip, teasing and good humour leaven the repetitive hard work.

Lattice and strap work

Most days there will be a variety of pots to deal with, and today is no exception. This morning, Liz is busy turning plain pots with heavy rims and heavy footrings round their base into fancy baskets. First, she slips a plug of hard-ish clay into the barrel of a wall-mounted extruder. Then, by pulling hard down on the extruder's handle, she can force the clay out through a template cut to give ridged strips. These she will stick to the side of the pots, first on one diagonal, then on the other, to create a lattice effect loosely reminiscent of a basket. Finally, the rim is 'rusticated' by running a roulette around it, a tool like a toothed cog which can spin around on the end of a wooden handle.

Below: Patterned roulettes are used while the pot is still on the wheel – the clay or brass wheel is pressed into the pot as it turns gently for one revolution.

Above: Attention to detail and a keen eye are needed for freehand decoration.

Rachel is applying similar strapwork, but to a much larger pot. Her strips are plain and, although pressed on to the pot by hand, as with the smaller pots, they are also subjected to the extra pressure of a special roulette rolled over them to give the desired ridged effect. This is quite a new technique that was developed to counter the tendency for strapwork to peel off the pot after frosts. I have never seen, for example, an Edwardian basket pot of the kind so loved by Gertrude Jekyll with a complete set of straps. One of our big basket pots will take over an hour to decorate in this manner, an act of meticulous perseverance.

Sprig moulds

Apart from the baskets, there are all manner of sprig moulds that are applied to different pots, adding low-relief design. An original design is modelled on to the side of a pot and then cast in plaster of Paris. This cast can then be offered up to other similar pots. As the moulds are usually shallow, the inside wall of the pot can be pushed out into the mould. Then, when taken away, it reveals an imprint of the original motif on the side of the pot.

If the mould is very deep, it may need to be partially filled with clay before being offered up to the pot. However, where possible, no clay is added so that the decoration and pot are all one homogeneous piece of clay and cannot be parted either by the strains of drying or the frost.

In this way, simple pots become covered with swags, sprout satyrs' heads, or have some family motif emblazoned on their side. Many designs are derived from flowers or leaves, the most successful being bold, easily recognisable shapes such as hosta leaves, fritillaries or arum lilies. Too much detail does not suit our modern tastes and also can distract the eye from the important other half of a flowerpot – the plantings.

This morning, Liz has been having trouble creating an even spacing between her basketware and the diamond-shaped gaps are all lopsided. Since everything is done by eye, it takes some time before angles and gaps come to be judged correctly. I suggest a lower chair or higher work level, which will alter her eye level and help her posture. With such a physically demanding job, best use of the body is very important to help in avoiding bad backs.

What is it that attracts apprentices to Whichford? Sometimes it is the prospect of a local job as part of a convivial team, but often it is the desire to learn our particular speciality, the skill of throwing. My final call this morning is to the other large workroom reached by walking the gangway between the kiln-drying pots. There I find the other two apprentices, Joe and Adam, my son, both keen to learn the tricks of throwing large pots on the wheel.

Facing page: A mould of decorative detail is offered up to the wall of a pot (above) which is then pressed out into it using finger and thumb. The mould is removed (below) revealing the decoration – a handle between stylised lily flowers. Made from the wall of the pot itself, it can never be forced off by frost.

Above: The shelves of our design library are stacked with decorative moulds and their rubber master copies.

Ours is a very ancient craft. The wheel was invented somewhere in Mesopotamia (an area roughly covered by modern Iraq), sometime towards the end of the third millennium BC, and was almost immediately used to make pots. This represented a huge techno-logical innovation for potters – even on the most primitive of wheels, you can produce 60, maybe 100 small, rough pots in an hour, compared with only a handful if you are using the more ancient method of hand-building.

The wheel allows for mass production, which means surplus and the growth of trade. Together with stone axehead production from centres like Grimes Graves, a neolithic flint mine in Norfolk, those early Mesopotamian potters were the first to establish the pattern of specialist workshops. They lived by trading their surpluses, the basis of modern capitalist society. At the same time, writing in clay was developed, enabling records of trading deals to be made. Soon, metallurgy would develop in the ore-rich hills to the north in Anatolia, and it is reasonable to assume that the potters' skills with fire and kilns was an important element in that.

The simplest wheel is still used in India, shown here in a 19th-century photograph. A round stone slab is set spinning like a child's top using a stick. The momentum thus generated allows the potter to centre his clay.

Wheel throwing has always flourished in times of peace, prosperity or cultural sophistication, and has often died out in times of social upheaval. Roman Britain was full of superb, delicate, wheel-made pottery, both from home and abroad. However, the archaeological evidence shows that after the legions left, local potteries either ceased production altogether or reverted to making small numbers of rough, hand-coiled pots.

Not until the economic resurgence of the 12th century AD is the wheel used again with any skill. In this respect, the fortunes of pottery and gardening weave in and out of time together. It seems creativity can only be expressed in such tangible forms in times of peace and prosperity.

The first wheel

The simplest and earliest form of the potter's wheel acts on the principle of a child's spinning top. I have seen wheels like this still in use in West Bengal, the sharp tip of their stubby axle spinning in a groove on the face of a white quartz pebble. I do not have the knack of using such a wheel, which requires perfect symmetry of force to be applied to the clay from both hands to avoid the wheel lurching sideways and then careering off across the floor at an alarming speed.

More sophisticated wheels have a short axle poking down under the wheel, enabling a pair of simple greased wooden bearings to hold the axle and its wheel firm. In that way, you can exert pressure on one side only. Indeed, it is the energetic tension between the even centrifugal force and the unevenness begun and followed through by the thrower which becomes the force that makes the pot grow.

All wheels must rotate, because it is the bringing to bear of that kinetic energy on to the lump of clay through the potter's hands that begins to form a pot. The heavier the lump of clay, or bigger the pot aimed for, the more energy is needed.

The flywheel

Often wheels have heavy wheelheads or flywheels. Once spun up to speed, both of these hold extra energy. In India, China, and Japan (where they throw anticlockwise), the motive power is usually provided by a stick. This is deftly located in a socket on the outside of the slowing wheel and pushed around a few times until speed is increased. The larger the pot, the more interruptions needed in throwing to regain speed.

In the Middle East and Europe a different system evolved. The wheelhead was raised and the potter sat on a bench (rather than on the floor). This allowed his legs to run along a floor-level solid flywheel, kicking it around. This type of wheel is still common all over Europe, the French ones having a flywheel about 1.2m (4ft) wide.

In England, at about the time of the Industrial Revolution, a final sophistication was added. By inserting a U-shaped bend into the axle just above the flywheel, a kickbar could be attached and used by the left foot. This enabled a top-up of circular motion at every revolution with a gentle kick that could be done as the thrower continued to form the clay, except for the very biggest pots.

At the same time, a counter shaft geared 3:1 was added below the wheelhead. This allowed three revolutions of the pot for every one of the main shaft and kickbar. This is ideal for small pots that only use the very centre of the wheel where the revolutions are the slowest. It was on this design of wheel that I trained at Wrecclesham. For the first five years as a professional potter, I only threw on kickwheels.

Nowadays, however, the motive power at Whichford comes not from the leg, but variable speed electric motors. These are controlled by the left foot which previously would have spent a very tiring day kicking. The romantic in me cries 'Shame!', but I do not miss the aches and pains. I agree with William Morris's dictum that technology can properly be used to relieve drudgery as long as the cutting edge of manufacture remains the skilled hand.

For every different kind of wheel, there is a variation in throwing technique. At Whichford, I teach the Wrecclesham style, but all traditional styles have much in common. Watching a good thrower is like watching a dancer as he measures out his movements with shifting balance and speed, following the prescribed choreography

An old kickwheel that I built poses for its photograph in the valley above Whichford. It is based on a 19th-century English design, where a kickbar and crank rotate a shaft kept spinning by a heavy flywheel.

with elegant and economical precision. In our style of throwing there are a set number of moves, honed down to the bare essentials by many generations.

I check that Joe and Adam are not having any technical problems – which hand to put where and when – but I cannot give them that dancer's sense of rhythm and timing. They will pick it up more intuitively from working alongside the more experienced throwers. Eventually they will develop their own sense of pace, of when to exert muscle to start something new and when to merely guide the turning momentum of the evolving pot.

Does everyone have the same rhythm? Of course not: but in all creation there has to be that necessary balance between assertive and passive, whatever the personal style.

The rain has gone now and a bitter wind is wiping away the ragged clouds. The air is changing and we will have frost tonight. I am outside, helping to move around our display pots in preparation for our Winter Sale. At this event, we have lectures with soup and braziers outside, and many come along to admire the garden.

When positioning a pot, it is helpful to decide whether it needs to play an active or a passive role. Am I expecting this pot to shout loudly, act as a focal point and draw attention to itself by its colourful antics? Or is it quietly adding detail, helping to emphasise a point or adding a supportive background by filling up some gap?

The situation will usually suggest a space to be filled and the general lines to be followed. The round shoulders of an ali baba can be used to soften hard edges of walls or paths, while the angles of a sharper, squarer design will seem to tighten up a rambling corner.

An important consideration is height. Even after I have decided on a pot to use, I will often try it out at different levels by propping the pot on layers of loose bricks or upturned plain pots. A flowerpot on the ground is often, literally, overlooked, and lifting it up will help it to gain visual importance and act as a resting point for the eye.

Our entrance pathway is flanked by formal lines of pots, which create an expectation by leading the eye towards the main garden. The arch at the far end of the path frames a single pedestal urn. This has had to be raised up on three layers of bricks so that it fills the whole of the lower part of the archway. It acts as a focal point in what would otherwise be an asymmetrical mixture of flowerbed and paving. The shape of the arch demands a tall shape to answer it and, with strong planting, the urn draws the eye to it.

However, with lines of pots, it is the repetition that is important rather than individual identity. In previous years, three pairs of plain shapes gave a sober and formal feel, whereas this year we are experimenting with different designs, sizes and heights for each pair.

Both concepts work visually in their own way, although the plain pots seemed to demand the sobriety of carefully clipped box balls. The pairs of pots we have used this year provide an altogether richer fare. They require more complicated mixed plantings that become darker in colour as they progress from the first arch.

Left: Two ways to create a focal point. This large area of gravel needs to be broken up, especially in winter when the borders to either side are empty. Above, an antique seakale forcer takes pride of place, guarded by feathery sentinels of *Stipa tenuissima*. Below, the same pot forms part of a still life of garden equipment, sculpture and even a salt-glazed stormwater trap.
Facing page: Repetition leads the eye along and away, transforming a narrow town passageway with tufts of different grasses and colourful heuchera.

Elsewhere, we have already cleared away a great deal of dead and half-dead plants. These include the half-hardy bedding plants that we had no room for in the greenhouse and that have been killed by the late autumn frosts. There is much tipping out of spent and root-matted compost from pots. This will be barrowed and spread on the vegetable garden where it helps to improve the heavy clay soil.

The empty pots are mostly returned to our stack of weathered and much-used pots – pots of every conceivable shape and size. A few favourites may be left in situ, but I prefer the radical clear-up that winter encourages, leaving you a clean sheet with which to stimulate new ideas.

We have also sorted out our 'borderline' plants. We have a couple of venerable agaves, *A. americana*, which, in theory, might survive outside in a sheltered position. However, we err on the side of

caution and at least take them into the polytunnel, or put them under the benches at the cooler end of the greenhouse where they lurk and tear at the flesh of the unwary gardener.

Cordylines are usually left outside, as Issy has perfected a method of trussing up their outer leaves to protect the inner growing point. She binds them into a bundle with colourful dogwood stems. We also have three fair-sized tree ferns, *Dicksonia antarctica*, which are usually brought into the polytunnel in their large terracotta pots and wrapped in fleece. Straw or old fern fronds are used to protect their crowns. One of them, though, recently spent a couple of winters in a warm corner of my walled garden quite happily.

Above: Early morning frost glints on pots that have been decorated with a crimped pastry design.
Facing page: Phormium is an invaluable New Zealand plant for mid-winter displays. The strong, clean shape of the pot, finished to a warm cream colour, offers an ideal foil to the unruly planting above.

choosing a location

Above: The last sun catches yellow witch hazel flowers (*Hamamelis* x *intermedia* 'Pallida'). The show only lasts for two weeks, so we move the pot centre stage.

Careful consideration of site is important with plants that may get frost damaged. *Osteospermum jucundum* survives as two huge cushions in a sunny, raised border in the pottery courtyard, but we would hesitate to plant it anywhere more exposed. With plants in pots, however, we can experiment with different sites. For instance, we can move fluffy grass seed-heads and large pansies out of the wind to stop them being shredded. Sempervivums can be put in the lee of larger pots or placed on window-sills to stop them from getting waterlogged, while *Lewisia cotyledon* hybrids can be put on their sides to prevent water from collecting in their rosettes.

Some plants that flower in the spring, such as camellias, must not be placed in an east-facing position because their buds will be defrosted too quickly by the morning sunshine. Several useful evergreens, such as *Elaeagnus pungens* 'Maculata' and *Garrya elliptica*, similarly resent facing east or being exposed to freezing winds that scorch their leaves. So, as winter progresses, some displays may be shuffled in order to protect the plants, hide casualties and keep things interesting. We never feed during the winter, but may need to water if there is a long dry spell, as long as there is no frost due.

Left: No attempt is made to soften the harshness of this concrete paving. Rather, its geometry is harnessed in a simple arrangement using stainless steel and bronze, with both metals echoed in the leaves of the heucheras.

Above: It may be too cold to sit on your garden seats in winter, but they make ideal show benches for flowerpots.

We construct our new winter plantings in the same way as those of any other season. A good layer of broken crocks is laid in the base of the pot to stop the compost from being washed out of the drainage hole and to prevent waterlogging. In very large pots (or if weight is a problem as on balconies or roof gardens) we substitute broken polystyrene seedboxes for the crocks, sometimes to a depth of 23cm (9in) if that will allow sufficient volume of compost for root growth.

I do not like to use gravel, as we find that it can become quickly clogged with repeated watering. Neither, incidentally, do we use pot feet. To me, they are a visual impediment and it is very rare to find a surface smooth and level enough, or a pot unmoved for such a long period of time that a waterproof seal is made beneath it.

Next, we fill the pot with fresh compost, leaving a space from the top that is the depth of the plant's rootball. When doing a mixed planting, we arrange the plants together, still in their plastic pots, so that we can try different combinations and patterns. When we are satisfied, we take the whole lot out and put them on the ground in the same pattern. Then, starting with the largest rootball, we remove each in turn from its plastic pot and put it in its position, finally filling any gaps between rootballs with compost. We avoid firming up the potting compost unnecessarily – watering will do that soon enough and air is essential for root growth. Even in winter, we give everything a good soaking when we have finished, finally checking for any crevices that have opened up in the compost and filling them up.

If we are using our very big pots for annual displays, we do not replace all the compost every year, but dig out the top 38cm (15in). We fork in a little blood, fish and bonemeal into the remainder, then top up with fresh compost. We only replace the whole volume every three years. I know some gardeners who blanch at the number of bags of compost needed for our biggest pots, and fill the lower half with ordinary garden compost, and this can work perfectly well.

When it comes to choosing plants, winter is a special season. In most parts of England, and certainly at Whichford, we only use plants that can withstand hard frosts. As well as limiting what we can consider choosing, frosts also prevent new growth. So, do not expect winter plantings to fill up as with the other seasons: what you have as you finish planting must already look filled out.

In any complex planting, be it large or small, I follow the same principles. I divide my choice of plants into three categories to establish the form and structure of the planting. First, I choose the centrepiece, which must, above all, have height. Second, I surround this with a 'midriff' of upright plants of medium height. And, thirdly, I choose low-growing or trailing plants to go against the rim, fitting in below the midriff. In this way, I construct a pyramid of plants.

These principles need to be adapted according to the proposed position of the pot. If I am designing for a spot against a wall, the centrepiece will be put at the back to start with, rather than in the middle for an all-round position. Some plants may be of so strong a colour or form that they need to be balanced by a compensating asymmetry, a larger area of less attention-grabbing plants. Like all rules in gardening, my ones for plantings are a useful guide, but sometimes need to be broken.

taking shape

As the gaudy colours of summer and autumn fade to a distant memory, the shapes of the plants that you choose for winter become more and more important. Topiary is a highly addictive way of imposing form on plants and our growing collection of box trained into balls, standards, mini hedges, cones and blobs really comes into its own in winter. *Buxus sempervirens* actually grows as a rare native in the woods around here, however I am much more used to seeing it on the parched hillsides of scrubby maquis in Haute Provence. There it grows in the mountains, up at a height of nearly 1,525m (5,000ft), and it is quite used to serious winters and precious little soil, so thrives in flowerpots.

Making simple topiary out of box requires only the idea, a sharp pair of secateurs and patience, for box is a slow grower. I have kept a box square in a 30cm (12in) pot for 12 years now. Each year I pull it out of its pot in late autumn or early winter for a thorough root-prune and general banging about to release spent compost, before returning it to the same pot surrounded by fresh compost and giving it a good watering.

I treat larger specimens in the same way. If I need to plant a really enormous pot, I will often use one of them as a centrepiece, but leave it in its own container which I either partially or wholly plunge into the centre of the compost of the bigger pot. I recommend this method for any larger shrub or small tree included in a very large planting as it contains the root growth of the shrub, making it much easier to disassemble the planting at the end of its time.

Lonicera nitida (especially the bright 'Baggesen's Gold'), golden privet and holly are also useful candidates for topiary. Bay lollipops look traditionally good in our pots, but we have found that the icy winter winds that whip down the valley and funnel through the courtyard do not agree with them. Topiary looks good by itself in pots, but we often insert some winter-flowering violas or primulas around its toes.

The strong shapes of topiary come into their own in the winter. On the facing page, a box exclamation mark finishes the argument between a variegated ivy, the grass *Carex buchananii*, and *Skimmia japonica*. Below, simple box balls measure out the path from the pottery.

Above: The Romans invented the art of topiary, and strong, tall shapes in box have been part of Italian gardening ever since.

Facing page: The tall shape of a longtom supports an unruly mass of grass hair: *Stipa arundinacea* gives height and *Carex* 'Evergold' spills over the rim. Purple heuchera complete a planting that will look good several years running.

height and form

For winter, my choice as a centrepiece will usually be an evergreen. Fastigiate (upright) evergreens, for example a grey-green juniper, make good strong verticals, as do phormiums and cordylines. *Phormium tenax* creates huge – up to 1.5 or 1.8m (5 or 6ft) – exclamation marks in greens or purples, and some usually smaller, varieties such as *P*. 'Maori Sunrise' come in jolly pink and green stripes. If we are feeling bold, height can be emphasised by missing out midriff plants completely. Instead the centrepiece can be surrounded with low-growing plants (*Ajuga reptans*, sedums, *Vinca minor*…) and a sheet of crocuses buried below, waiting to take over in the New Year.

Other major plants with strong silhouettes include mahonias (*M. aquifolium* 'Apollo' is one of the smaller ones; save *M*. x *media* 'Charity' for a very large pot), and fragrance is a bonus here. The criss-cross arrangement of hebe leaves is somehow more

noticeable now, when flowers are absent. *Juniperus squamata* 'Blue Star' will sprawl sideways out of a pot – very useful when you feel a little asymmetry is needed.

The overwintering stems of euphorbias can provide tall or middle-height interest with their bold rosettes of leaves. Some are upright (*Euphorbia characias*), or tinged with purple (*E. amygdaloides* 'Rubra'), while others are glaucous and sprawling (*E. myrsinites*).

Do not be afraid to cheat if your plantings need extra height. We raid the garden for red or acid-green cornus stems, and plant them like porcupine quills at the back of, or through, the rest of the plants. You can also use the white stems of *Rubus thibetanus* if your skin is thick – beware the prickles. We have also been known to beg bits of contorted willow or hazel from neighbours – with any luck these hardwood cuttings will root and can be potted up when the arrangement is dismantled in a few months' time. We sometimes spray the more boring twigs with colours picked up from other flowers or foliage in the planting, or go for festive silver or gold as Christmas looms on the horizon.

Form is often naturally intriguing, as in the horizontals of *Lonicera pileata* or the barmy corkscrews of *Juncus effusus* f. *spiralis*, and a plant with striking shape makes an excellent starting point for a planting. You may also choose a major or minor plant for the shape of its individual leaves, for example, crinkly *Pittosporum tenuifolium* or *Hedera helix* 'Parsley Crested'.

Many fillers come into this group. Semi-evergreen and evergreen ferns, such as *Polystichum setiferum* and *Polypodium vulgare*, have a feathery quality that is rare at this time of year, and good old Hart's Tongue (*Asplenium scolopendrium*) pokes its bold, shiny blades out for most of the year wherever you put it. The quilted foliage of *Viburnum davidii* provides an interesting foil for more upright plants.

In winter we have to look harder to find colour, but are always rewarded by coming across it unexpectedly in stems or in details, like the red rims on the discreet green cups of *Helleborus foetidus*. We have a handsome rust-tinted ivy that is trained around an ironwork globe. Nobody notices it in the chaos of summer, but it does attract lots of comment in the quieter winter. This season can seem a dull time of year, but it does force you to study the whole plant rather than just relying on the colourful baubles of summer flowers.

Variegated leaves are particularly useful in winter and can brighten up any dull corner, glinting in the low winter sunlight. *Euonymus fortunei* 'Silver Queen' and *E. f.* 'Emerald 'n' Gold' may scream 'Car parks!' to you. Yet, put them in a handsome pot placed next to a wall so that they can start to scramble upwards, and in darkest December you will be sorry that you were so rude about them. Variegated ivies are not to be sniffed at either, for the same reason. Beefier variegated plants include *Elaeagnus pungens* 'Maculata', *Aucuba japonica* 'Crotonifolia' and, of course, many hollies, such as *Ilex* x *altaclerensis* 'Golden King' or *I. aquifolium* 'Ferox Argentea', which is not only variegated but has a mad proliferation of spines all over its leaves.

Grey leaves, useful in summer for toning down garish colours, are even more closely studied in winter, and *Ballota pseudodictamnus* and *Stachys byzantina* are still strokeable on dry days. Neatly clipped santolina or lavender can give satisfying shape and useful lightness. *Festuca glauca* 'Elijah Blue' makes handy little tuffets to soften up a planting. We even find that *Senecio cineraria* 'Silver Dust' is hardy enough to get through some winters here at Whichford. Grey combines especially well with purple (heucheras are extremely useful fillers), with *Salvia officinalis* 'Purpurascens' and *S. o.* 'Tricolor' bridging the two colours nicely. Do not throw away excess purple ajugas from the garden – use them as underplantings in containers.

Above: These subtle, rusty colours are overlooked in other seasons, but suit this calm winter day, picking up the earthy colours of the frescoes behind.
Facing page: This heather will keep its colour throughout the winter while the hyacinth leaves gradually push through from below. The thin strands of *Carex buchananii* wave to and fro in the slightest breeze, kept in some order by cut stems of Cornus pushed into the soil to add extra interest.

Berries and flowers

Berries carry the fruitfulness of autumn into winter, as long as they are spared by the birds. As well as hollies, many cotoneasters and pyracanthas are perfectly happy in large pots. Symphoricarpos, a tiresome sucker producer in most situations, can be usefully confined in a pot and will live up to its common name 'Snowberry'. Plant something tough and vigorous (*Euphorbia robbiae, Ajuga reptans* perhaps) to fill the gaps between its stems.

Gaultheria mucronata 'Wintertime' will provide more white berries, whereas *G. m.* 'Mulberry Wine' will have you running around looking for purple foliage to pick up on its magenta-purple fruit. Both of these will need ericaceous compost. If you have spare *Iris foetidissima*, it is worth jamming some into a purplish planting where those bright orange seeds will shine out and wake up the more sombre colours.

Skimmia japonica is well known for the berries it produces (as long as both male and female plants are around). But, in winter plantings it is also useful for its rusty red panicles of flower buds, echoed in *S. j.* 'Rubella' by the red edges of its leaves. There are handsome greenish white-flowered versions, too, which look delicious with *Primula vulgaris* or miniature narcissi. Be careful later, however: skimmias do not like to be parked in scorching sunshine during the summer.

Flowers at this bare time of year stand out, and can stop you in your tracks. The winter-trained eye easily spots the yellow witch hazel or pink *Viburnum* x *bodnantense* flowers – probably before your nose has even started twitching, so their fragrance is a bonus. However, *Sarcococca confusa* has people whiffling about like hedgehogs ('Where is that lovely smell coming from?'). *Daphne mezereum* and *Lonicera* x *purpusii* waft around the corner to meet you even before you have come through the garden gate.

Viburnum tinus 'Gwenllian' and *V. t.* 'Eve Price' are both good-tempered, rounded evergreen shrubs which will flower through most of winter. A long-flowering perennial that is happy jammed around the roots of these is *Pulmonaria rubra*, which can be in flower by Christmas and will carry on through the spring. Hellebores – from the tasteful (but prone to sudden death) white *H. niger* to the pinks, whites, purples, blacks, spots, streaks and even doubles of *Helleborus hybridus* – are useful medium-height flowerers with strong foliage. It is kinder to release them into the garden after a potted season, which gives you an excuse to buy more next year! For the more frugal, they are easy to grow from fresh seed, as long as you are not fussy about the exact shade of the seedlings' flowers.

Above: Glass beads glued to wire stalks sprout from a clump of sempervivum like some strange winter fruit. The pot is affectionately known as a Flying Saucer. Facing page: The flowers of a male *Skimmia japonica* 'Rubella' are complemented by the berries of the low-growing *Skimmia japonica* ssp. *reevesiana*.

We could not do without the enormous range of winter-flowering violas for underplanting and gap filling. We order them as plug plants in early July, and pot them on in the greenhouse when they arrive in late August. This year we had a fantastic glowing blue and orange one that we think was called *V.* 'Moonlight', although we often find that we cannot get the same ones repeatedly. Anyway, it is more fun trying some new ones each year.

The only one that we really do buy regularly is an exotic frilly one called 'Flamenco' which starts to flick its skirts in the earliest mild spells. The smaller violas, such as 'Jackanapes', almost always give excellent value right up to Chelsea, and are often a bit hardier than the bigger ones and less damaged in wet weather.

Many people consider themselves too sophisticated for the sweet-shop colours of primulas, but we do not! If you really cannot stand the bright blues and reds, good old *Primula vulgaris* and its lookalikes seem to be available practically all winter. They tone beautifully with the yellow variegation on hollies and euonymus or elaeagnus. *Primula* Wanda Group provides lovely glowing red and purple, jewel-like colours, and it is more weatherproof than some of the flashier types you will see in garden centres. Just one or two of these in a planting will bring out colours in the leaves, petioles and stamens of other plants that you had not noticed before.

Nothing wipes away the late winter blues like the sight of *Crocus tommasinianus*, or one of the many species of snowdrop boring through the frost-encrusted compost. Mini narcissus – 'February Gold', 'Jetfire', 'Jack Snipe', for example – come up early, too, starting off the springtime yellows, and we often shove a few of these under our winter plantings. Forced bulbs in pots also cheer us up in the winter. We always bring on some hyacinths, narcissi such as 'Paper White', and hippeastrums to brighten up the office, gallery and the pottery, especially now we have plenty of glazed planters to show off.

Outside, hyacinths start coming up surprisingly early for such big, fleshy things. They work well in bigger, bolder plantings (although there are some surprisingly subtly coloured ones) or on their own in small terracotta pots. These can be set on window-sills or can be used to fill unplanned gaps in bigger plantings.

Above: The lush colours of *Hyacinthus orientalis* 'Delft Blue' and *H.* 'Woodstock' shout that spring will soon be here, and their lavish scent fills the room.
Facing page: A pot of *Crocus tommasinianus* to bring inside midwinter.

Talking of unplanned gaps, in autumn it is worth having planted plenty of spare bulbs in odd plastic pots, ready to magic into the hole left by some unexpected death. However many of these late winter bulbs you plant in the autumn, in January you will be wishing you had bought twice as many.

Winter aconites (*Eranthis hyemalis*) can be bought 'in the green' (that is sold as non-flowering plants). They actually prefer to be transplanted in this way, as do snowdrops.

The other invaluable corm that can be bought as a small plant is *Cyclamen coum*, with flowers from white to carmine pink. They have prettily marked, rounded leaves which, on pink-flowered plants, are backed with dark pink. All of these are ideal candidates for last-minute bunging-in to rejuvenate a planting whose lower storey lacks a little something, and survive quite happily in the shade of large evergreens.

Small early iris, such as the reticulata types, prefer a well-drained compost and are shown off better simply planted with nothing more than a mini sedum around their feet, or just some neat gravel. *I.* 'Katharine Hodgkin' is horribly expensive, but worth it for the subtly marked blue and yellow flowers. *I. unguicularis* varieties emerge right through the winter, depending on where you are, but need a sheltered position. All these little irises need protecting from slugs and a raised position on a wall or window-sill will help with this while allowing closer inspection of their progress.

Below: Tiny *Iris* 'Katharine Hodgkin' win the race on my windowsill, starting a two-month procession of indoor winter bulbs.

You can pick up colours with glass nuggets or even bottles – anything, really, as long as it is relatively weatherproof, and in touch with your chosen colours and style. I draw the line at the old farm machinery, although rusty iron and terracotta do go well together, and I have used a beautiful dusty-blue wooden barrow before now, but I prefer to use wackiness with some caution. Like serious colour clashes, the occasional shock in the garden adds interest and focus, but too much together just creates an unrelated mess, or certainly requires a much greater degree of skill to bring off the effect successfully.

But it is getting too cold for all that now. And too late. The sky is clear, the wind has veered to the north and is now dropping. The sunset is tinged with the sharp green that heralds clear, frosty weather. Later in the year we will be working long hours, but now our homes beckon and we shout our goodbyes to each other through the curling smoke of our breath.

I fill a basket with beech logs and stomp indoors, a long evening lies ahead in front of the fire and I will think of the changes that we have made today, the new plant combinations discovered, planning, dreaming…

Above: A pair of bantams shelter from the winter winds in the courtyard.

Props for pots

If a planting looks rather sparse or there are gaps where bulbs are waiting to perform, we often dress the space with a motley collection of props that we keep to hand – interesting stones, old horse shoes, sea shells, empty pots laid on their sides, lions' mask wall plaques. All of these will fill spaces until either the evergreen plants plump up in the early spring or the bulbs start to come up. If you have used heavy stones or bits of intriguing ironmongery, it is, however, essential to remove them before emerging bulbs get all bent out of shape trying to force their way around them.

Above: Props come into their own during the sparse winter months. Lengths of old lead pipe decorated with blue glass beads twine around a simple planting of pansies and rosemary.

Many of these will be useful all year round or will continue well into spring; most of them have interesting evergreen foliage.

Perennials

Ajuga reptans 'Atropurpurea', 'Multicolor' **PS**

Asplenium scolopendrium **PS; R; WD**

Euphorbia amygdaloides 'Rubra' **PS** (sap may cause skin irritation)

Festuca glauca 'Elijah Blue' **S; WD**

Hedera helix (many varieties) **S**

Helleborus corsicus **S–PS; R**

H. foetidus **R; S–Sh**

H. hybridus **R; S–PS**

H. niger **R; S–PS**

Heuchera 'Chocolate Ruffles', 'Palace Purple', 'Plum Pudding', 'Silver Streak' **S–PS**

Iris foetidissima **S–PS; WD**

Juncus effusus f. *spiralis* **S; T** (likes very wet soil)

Ophiopogon planiscapus 'Nigrescens' **S–PS; T; WD**

Phormium tenax **R; S–PS; WD**

Polypodium vulgare **PS–Sh; WD**

Polystichum setiferum **S–Sh; WD**

P. munitum **S–Sh; WD**

Pulmonaria rubra **PS–Sh; R**

Senecio cineraria 'Silver Dust' **M; S–PS**

Vinca major 'Variegata' **PS–Sh**

Vinca minor **PS–Sh**

Bedding

Brassica oleracea (ornamental cabbage) **R; S; T**

Primula vulgaris **R; S–PS; WD**

Primula Wanda Group **R; S–PS; WD**

Viola – any! We especially like 'Flamenco' and 'Jackanapes' **R; S–PS; WD**

Bulbs

Crocus chrysanthus ('Cream Beauty', etc) **S; WD**

C. vernus 'Pickwick' **S–PS; WD**

Cyclamen coum **PS; R; WD**

Eranthis hyemalis **S–PS**

Galanthus nivalis **PS–Sh**

Hyacinthus orientalis eg 'Gipsy Queen', 'Delft Blue', 'Woodstock'.
   P; S–PS; WD

Iris reticulata ('George', 'Cantab', 'Katharine Hodgkin' etc) **S; WD**

Narcissus bulbocodium. **S–PS; T; WD**

N. 'February Gold', Jetfire', 'Jack Snipe' etc **S–PS; WD**

N. 'Rip van Winkle' **S–PS; T; WD**

Alpines/miniatures

Sedum obtusatum **S; WD**

S. spathulifolium **S; WD**

Thymus x *citriodorus* 'Aureus', 'Silver Posie' **P; S; WD**

Evergreen shrubs

Buxus sempervirens **R; S–PS**

B. sempervirens 'Suffruticosa' **S–PS; WD**

Daphne laureola ssp. *philippi* **S–PS** (sap may irritate skin)

D. odora 'Aureomarginata' **P; S–PS**

Eleagnus pungens 'Maculata' **S–PS**

Erica carnea **E; S; WD**

Euonymus fortunei 'Silver Queen' and 'Emerald 'n' Gold' **S–PS**

Fatsia japonica **R; S–PS**

Gaultheria mucronata 'Wintertime' (f), 'Mulberry Wine' (f) – need a male for berry production, eg 'E.K. Balls'(!) **E; PS; T**

Garrya elliptica **S–PS**

Ilex x *altaclerensis* 'Golden King'(f) **S–PS**

I. aquifolium eg 'Ferox Aurea'(m), 'Golden Queen'(m),'Madame Briot'(f) **S–PS**

Juniperus squamata 'Blue Star' **S–PS**

Lonicera nitida 'Baggesen's Gold' **R; S–PS**

L. pileata **R; S–PS**

Mahonia aquifolium 'Apollo' **P; PS–Sh; R**

Pittosporum tenuifolium **S**

Salvia officinalis 'Purpurascens' and 'Tricolor' **S; WD**

Sarcococca confusa **P; PS–Sh**

Skimmia japonica eg 'Rubella' (m), 'Wakehurst White' (f) **PS–Sh; R**

Viburnum davidii (need m and f for berry formation) **R; S–PS**

V. tinus eg 'Eve Price' or 'Gwenllian' **R; S–PS**

Deciduous shrubs

Corylus avellana **R; S–PS; T**

Daphne mezereum **P; R; S–PS; WD**

Hamamelis mollis **P; S–PS**

Lonicera x *purpusii* **P; R; S–PS**

Key

E:	Prefers ericaceous compost
F:	Interesting foliage
M:	Survives mild winters outside with good drainage. If in doubt take insurance cuttings.
P:	Scented foliage or flowers
PS–Sh:	Thrives in partial shade or shade
R:	Likes a rich, fertile soil (add organic matter, such as leaf-mould)
S:	Prefers a sunny site
S–PS:	Will tolerate sun or partial shade
S–Sh	Happy with either sun or shade
Sh:	Thrives in a shady position
T:	Talking-point/attention-grabber – people will ask you what that plant is!
WD:	Requires a very well-drained soil that includes added grit or coarse sand.

Facing page: The extravagant crinolene of an ornamental winter cabbage.

spring

This early May morning, the shadows beneath the garden hedges are still pale with frozen dew, edged with a thin band of sparkling white as the sun moves in to melt the early morning frost. I go into the walled garden to remove the old coat I threw over my sprouting indigofera plant last night (I once nearly lost it to a late April frost that stripped its sap-swelled stems) and to admire the tulips. I can see the steep bank beside the woods a mile away just beginning to develop its blue sheen: the bluebells are coming and the cuckoo will not be far behind.

Spring is here! Summer is icumen in! I feel like singing with Gerard Manley Hopkins that

Nothing is so beautiful as spring –
     When weeds, in wheels, shoot long and lovely and lush;
Thrush's eggs look like little low heavens, and thrush
     Through the echoing timber does so rinse and wring
The ear, it strikes like lightnings to hear him sing;
     The grassy peartree leaves and blooms, they brush
The descending blue; that blue is all in a rush
     With richness; the racing lambs too have fair their fling.

All about me, the garden is bursting out of its hibernation. The lengthening days and heat from the sun crack open buds and draw the greenery out of the earth. What a joy! I am a practical illustration to Loudon's 1871 dictionary: 'Man, in common with most other animals indigenous with our climate, is generally in high spirits and vigour during May. Woe to the young gardener who exhausts his spirits in any other way than in self-improvement.' Ah, that Victorian propriety!

Left: After the drabness of winter, spring bulbs rush to proclaim the changing season and at their vanguard are the tulips. All tulips grow extremely well in flowerpots, where you can keep an eye on them as they grow and then move them out of sight to die back gracefully when they have finished flowering. These are all tall, late-flowering varieties, charmingly underplanted with a carpet of forget-me-nots.

Facing page: A pot sporting blue and pink mermaids inspired by Portmeirion shows banks of muscari, hyacinths and little 'Jack Snipe' narcissi breaking through a winter planting of pansies and ivies.

Still, I am no longer young, and the carpenter is here already and needs instruction on the Chelsea stand because, at Whichford, spring is the season of the Chelsea Flower Show. Of all the events that take place in the pottery year, this is the one that demands the most concentrated effort. After 20 such seasons of showing, I approach it with a mixture of excitement and dread.

The excitement comes from being part of the disparate community of garden designers, builders, craftsmen and viewing public who, together, make up this extraordinary happening. The whole enterprise is a form of sublime madness.

It is an exercise of imagination made incarnate that requires supreme efforts (and here's the dread) from teams of workers with the stamina to endure gruelling working conditions and excessively long hours; and all to be held at its supreme, polished best for five days precisely. Then, at the ringing of a handbell, it's all dismantled and destroyed. It is here that gardening becomes as ephemeral an art as that of cookery: one chance to taste the extraordinary and varied banquet, and then nothing remains but the memory.

There is a moment, felt, I think, by most designers who arrive at Chelsea to set up, when the whole experience threatens to overwhelm you. For months, if not years for the more ambitious displays, you have been pouring your creative best into fashioning a perfect jewel, a garden in miniature that has become a whole world in itself. And, suddenly, you are faced with your tiny plot of muddy grass, not alone, but beside many others, all being invested with a similar intensity of energy and ideas by their designers. At that moment, to facet your jewel so that it has a chance of flashing out amongst so many others seems a challenge indeed.

Facing page: The challenge at the annual Chelsea Flower Show is to fit an eye-catching display into a tiny space. Over the years, the Whichford stand has gone through many transformations. Here, snakes of stacked pots weave in and out between the plants.

Above: A carpet of small flowerpots and bright gazenias set off a riot of colourful annuals.

I have been exhibiting at Chelsea for over 20 years. My first time, it was just my father and I setting up, and we put down the hammer and nails with a quarter of an hour to spare before the Queen and her cavalcade swept into the grounds. Since those simple days, Whichford exhibits have become more complex, sometimes taking 600 hours just to erect, let alone to plan, plant and dismantle – a huge undertaking.

Our Chelsea displays are a team effort. We scout about for ideas all year, and the detailed planning has to start the moment we are allocated a site in the autumn. As in all garden design, the first consideration has to be the hard landscaping: how to divide the site up between paths and beds and make the most of the 'view' from key spots. We also have to plan some form of undercover space as our selling base – the weather in late English spring can be anything from bitter rain to burning sun.

Above: Sharp accents of blue and red provide focus in a jumble of pots.

We have been through many different styles over the years. Early on however, plants became an integral part of our displays. I soon began to see our restricted space as a tiny town garden and used it to try out different ideas.

A common feature has been the use of height – pots are banked up against the walls, or in free-standing pyramids, increasing the feeling of space by moving the eye upwards. We often choose a unified idea that runs right around the garden. One year, much use was made of blue glass bottles, dark blue and red painted pots, and glass beads. These were strung from trees, filled pots and even cascaded, instead of water, from overturned ali baba jars.

Another year, we used many New Zealand plants. Through a friend in the village, we imported crates of autumn gourds fresh from New Zealand and used them as props to dress elaborate mounds of antipodean plants, particularly phormiums, *Sansevieria trifasciata* and Tasmanian tree ferns. We also used many purple and orange flowers, a combination that has remained one of our favourites. The pots created a miniature mountain sprouting tree fern foliage. Screes of gourds cascaded down the many valley sides to the flat gravel sea below, itself harbouring the occasional group of flowerpot islands.

My usual design response to a small space is to make it seem larger by engaging the eye with lots of detail. This is not to everyone's taste, however, and at Chelsea I have also been through a minimalist phase, all gravel, tufts of grass, cut stone and stainless-steel poles, which was greatly appreciated by continental designers. The immediate stimulus was a new range of modern pots with a strong simple design that I had made. Yet, whilst I enjoyed the post-modernism as an exercise, I am too romantic a gardener for such simplicity, and too messy. I prefer the friendly chaos of complicated plantings that allow you the freedom to make changes whenever you want and to follow your whims.

By contrast, as design gets simpler, any deviation from the original concept begins to radically alter the balance of the whole. In ultra-modern and simple interiors, for instance, I am left feeling like one of those architect's drawings of a man in a suit with very pointed legs, worried lest I untidy a sofa. And I am certainly at a loss as to where I can put down the shopping without it shouting 'Mess!' at me while I have a cup of coffee. What, for some, is a peaceful, uncluttered living space, leaves me feeling dominated and insecure. Still, 'Vive la differénce!'

Below: In contrast, another year at Chelsea is all stainless steel and stone chic.

My inspiration for Chelsea this year came from a visit to Rome, a city where the romantic past and cutting-edge chic stand side by side and clash happily with one another. While there, I spent a long time examining and photographing old coloured walls. After some experimentation back home, painting raw pigment directly on to damp plaster, I came up with a dark Venetian red, edged in the dark brown of raw umber, as in Pompeian villas.

If we used this as a backdrop, I reasoned, our flowerpots would shine out against its darker tone. It would also suit our preferred colour range for the planting this year – greys and whites. This was to contrast with the previous year when we went a long way towards banishing green entirely by substituting all-purple foliage, a striking but sombre effect.

Creating the stand

We pre-build as much of our Chelsea stand as possible here, at Whichford. This morning, I walk over the road that runs along the front of the pottery and down the hill to what we grandly call the Design Studio. It's a series of buildings and shacks on the site of an old farmyard away from the main pottery site. Here we have the room to try out new ideas – and do messy jobs like constructing Chelsea paraphernalia.

I am going to use our very red backdrop to create a 'room' of red for us. I shall complete the effect by constructing a dividing wall right across the middle of the site, pierced by a huge Roman archway, complete with terracotta friezes and architraves.

While the carpenter measures, cuts and hammers, following my drawings, I am going to work on the terracotta friezes. On each side of the arch, a vase is to sprout a Tree of Life which will weave and twist upwards. It will be interrupted only by an acanthus-leaf capital from which the semi-circle of the archway will spring.

Most of our production at Whichford is made on the wheel. This is very effective for simple, round pots. However, if you want a square pot, a figurine, or a highly decorated tile, you need a different technique to make them – press moulding. For this, plaster moulds are used – these are taken off an original clay model that has been worked up by hand. Clay is pressed or beaten into the moulds and, in this way, many identical copies can be made relatively quickly.

Left and above: The Chelsea Flower Show often stimulates new ideas. This frieze was made especially to go with Pompeian-style frescoed walls. The tiles of the frieze are made by pressing clay into plaster of Paris moulds taken off clay originals.

Above: Vegetable labels made for HRH Prince Charles's shop at Highgrove – their press-moulded tips are embossed with his insignia.

To make the original tiles, I take a flat piece of clay and cut it to size. Then I model the design onto it, partly by cutting, partly by building up. These tiles are simple to make because they only need to be viewed from one angle. I prepare them quickly, building up the design freehand as I go along, mapping out only the central trunk of the Tree of Life which must meet up with the next tile. For the rest, I fill spaces with curling, upward moving branches and leaves. Then I dot some large, generic fruit around. Last, I work over the whole surface with a soft, wet paintbrush to even out the texture and calm down rough burrs.

Then comes the casting. I build a little wall of clay around the tile and mix a bucket of plaster. Just as it is beginning to stiffen, but is still the consistency of single cream, I pour it out so that it covers the model (it is stopped from flooding away by the wall of clay). After a few minutes, the plaster is hard enough to handle. The original is dug out and any undercuts – where the clay has got trapped under an overhang of plaster – are tidied up with a metal tool.

Later, I will take the mould back over the road and put it to dry over the kilns. The moulds for press moulding need to be dry before use because, when you first press and bang the clay into the mould, it will initially stick firm to the plaster. It is only after the dry plaster has sucked the stickiness out of the clay over a period of a few hours that the clay is released, allowing it to be turned out and another piece made.

I am also working on a more complicated casting of a garden sculpture. The most ancient press-moulded objects are small votive offerings of gods or animals placed in shrines, first in pre-dynastic Egypt, then all over the Near East and the Mediterranean. These were made from two-piece moulds as, unlike a tile, both front and back of the figures were visible and needed relief modelling.

I am going to use this simple method to make herms. These are figures that grow out of pillars. They were originally representations of the Roman god Terminus, guardian of boundaries, and were much-loved by the Landscape Movement in the 18th century. There are marvellous examples at West Wycombe in Buckinghamshire, and at Rousham, near here in north Oxfordshire.

Over the past couple of weeks, I have constructed a very simplified version of a herm, built up in solid clay around a metal pole for support. At this stage, it is minus arms and head. If this simple one is a success, I shall work up more elaborate, highly finished individuals. Some of the stone examples at West Wycombe hold baskets of fruit, and I like the idea of flowerpots full of cascading plants balanced on the heads, or held in the arms, of my planned terracotta versions.

Casting the herm

The figure will be much easier to cast lying down so, with Adam and Joe helping, we gingerly push it over backwards and lower it to the ground. Apart from a moment's panic when the ribcage starts to sag towards the floor – we save it by hurriedly pushing handfuls of clay under it as makeshift supports – all goes well, despite the great weight of the clay.

To produce the original easily, you make it in solid clay, cutting, modelling and carving, adding bits as you please. However, this heavy mass of clay would never survive the kiln as its extreme thickness would be sure to trap either air or water or both, making

it all-too likely to blow up when heated. Tiny figurines can be fired solid but larger ones have to be hollow, hence they are traditionally press-moulded.

Once our body is horizontal, we draw a line along his sides at the point where we want the mould to 'break' (to give two sections).

Then we construct a shelf coming straight out from the line to act as the face where the two halves will join. Around this shelf we build our wall, as with the tile, and then we are ready to mix and pour the plaster for the first half. Much care is also taken to ensure that the clay wall we have made for the liquid plaster is watertight, and it must be strong enough to hold the coming weight. If you spring a leak when pouring a big mould like this, the plaster can cascade out when your back is turned and set rock hard before you have time to clear it up.

With three of us on the job, this casting goes well. I enjoy the precision that you need to work with plaster: all the technicalities of building the case to hold the cast, the quiet moment when the buckets are mixed, waiting, and then the ordered rush. One person checks the mixes for that moment when liquid plaster announces its intention of changing state with a warming and thickening. The pourer anxiously looks out for leaks and the cleaner-up washes the plaster off the buckets in a fight against time before it sets irredeemably hard. A brief pause, then the walls are pulled away. For a moment, the still-soft plaster is like cheese and can be smoothed, slopped around and cut to shape if need be. In five minutes, it will be rock hard.

After tea break, we lever and heave the now doubly-heavy torso over on to its plaster-encased front. Its back is now revealed, rising out of its new plaster mattress. We brush the plaster ledge with soft soap to make a shiny buffer layer in order to prevent the next half sticking. Then we build a new clay wall and repeat the casting process over again.

Plaster casting is incurably messy. The plaster begins life as a fine dust, then there is the water and, when you have finished, all the waste walls and scrapings seem to get everywhere. Since the herm is a large piece, we have had to work right in the middle of the main studio, disturbing the peace of the other user of the space, my wife Dominique.

Facing page: More complex shapes can be press-moulded by using multi-piece plaster moulds, where each different part precisely follows the angles of the form. The mould for this figure is in three pieces.
Right: The finished herm provides a strong upright form, here punctuating a plain hedge at the end of a long vista.

Most large potteries in the past made a bit of everything, and we are no exception. Apart from our five children, Dominique and I also share in the making of glazeware. I throw the shapes based, as usual for me, on the European and Middle Eastern traditions. When they are leather hard (hard enough to handle without distorting), I dip the pots into a slip (liquid clay that is used for decoration and comes in a range of colours). This covers them in a thin coating of

Facing page: Pouring slip: most earthenware glazes show up better over white, applied in the form of a slip, made from white clays, flint and other ground rocks. Below: A slipware flower jug decorated by Dominique. She scratches her designs through half-dry slip to the dark body below, before painting on coloured glazes.

white clay. When this is almost dry, Dominique inscribes the pots with simple metal points or combs. She creates clear linear designs where the point of her tool breaks through the white surface layer into the darker colour of the original body.

Later, after they have been biscuit fired (like an ordinary flowerpot) she will paint simple colours over the decoration – greens from copper oxide and yellows from iron oxide – and then dip the whole pot once again, as with the slip, but this time into a glaze of powdered glass. A second firing and the pot is finished.

With Chelsea coming up, we are making a lot of jugs that provide excellent vases. This year, Dominique's imagination has covered them with wide-eyed owls, parrots flying through palm trees, plus many animals, acrobats and dancers chasing each other over rim and under handle. When I unload a glaze firing, I am always delighted by the inventive cavalcade cavorting around. And, as if in response, my normally solid repetition training breaks down when I throw them and I find an unexpected variety infiltrating each batch.

We have recently begun to make glazed flowerpots as well, especially in different shades of green. We've been playing with detailed relief panels, too, which sparkle under the rich, shiny texture. The pots are mostly small, ideal for holding a specimen plant on a window-sill, or good for pointing up a larger group of pots. We have also tried larger glazed flowerpots and they look especially good indoors or in a conservatory. In the garden, they make a very strong, unchanging statement – in most circumstances, I prefer the variability of terracotta.

To make up for the mess and noise of the casting, we load a small electric kiln for Dominique, setting the glazed pots on shelves. The glaze coating has dried to a brittle, dusty skin on the pots and must not be chipped. Neither must a pot touch anything else in the kiln. Otherwise, as the glaze powder melts, it will act as a glue.

spring-cleaning the greenhouse

Above: By late spring, the Whichford greenhouse is always bursting at the seams with tender bedding plants waiting to make up our summer displays.

After lunch, I work in the greenhouse that, in the spring, is very much the centre of our gardening activity. Icy winds can hurtle down this valley and the warmth of the gas heater is a good encouragement to begin the season's propagation early. This is all the more appealing when sleet is still rattling on the glass. The protection and gentle heat offered by the greenhouse are vital: we can nurture the many frost-sensitive species that we will use for our summer displays, encouraging them into early growth.

Our greenhouse is not grand, but it is large – about 9m (30ft) long – and sits between the packing shed and the stockyard. This means that its poor relation, a polytunnel squashed between the greenhouse and a hedge, is often the scene of territorial wrangles amongst gardeners and packers as dry storage gets scarce at the end of winter. At this time, both flowerpots and plants are building up before the exodus of April and May.

It is some time in February that the greenhouse begins its growing year. The ravages of winter will have left it looking somewhat moth-eaten, so we choose a relatively mild day and get ruthless, culling dead or dying plants. Many of these are last year's bedding

plants that have been kept out of curiosity to see if they will come through to make big plants for the summer, or will be vigorous enough to provide cuttings.

This year, the big fat blue *Verbena* x *hybrida* is looking promising, but *Bidens ferulifolia* and a dusty mauve osteospermum are hanging on by the skin of their teeth. These two did sterling work at Chelsea last year, but there is no room for sentimentality in our greenhouse and they are condemned to the compost heap. The survivors stand outside for the day or, if they are very sensitive, they're put in the polytunnel along with those stacks of pots that creep in to overwinter.

Now there is room for us to begin the general clean-out of the greenhouse. Mouldy cups of coffee are scraped out; scrawled notes, unidentifiable seed-heads, twigs, broken hose fittings… all are flung in the bin. Heaps of plastic pots are sorted into boxes, small clay pots brushed out and stacked on shelves. The gravel on the benches is raked and weeded, replenished if necessary, and we brush all along the aluminium struts of the greenhouse and under the benches in an attempt to dislodge any overwintering snails and vine weevils.

The glass is washed inside and out. Some years, we spray the whole thing down with Jeyes Fluid, a disinfectant. But, beneath the boxes of dahlia tubers and in the cracked earth under the benches lurk frogs, toads and newts – especially the juveniles for some reason. We would rather have them than sterile efficiency.

The chosen survivors are brought back in and lined up on the benches, with old leaves and straggly stems trimmed off as we go along. With the greenhouse tidy, the plants look greener already. We can take a deep breath and acknowledge that spring really is on its way, accelerating all the time. We must hurry if we want to keep up with it.

As I look round our Whichford greenhouse (of which I am quite proud), my musings are interrupted by an ear-splitting screech – Issy has found another caterpillar. For, as spring progresses and temperatures rise, it is not only the plants that wake up.

We cannot claim to garden entirely organically at Whichford, as we use slug pellets around mollusc favourites such as the delphiniums. However, we use them sparingly and it is usually only necessary to apply them once. Snails love to overwinter under clay pots so, as we tidy up we grab them by the handful and throw them over the hedge into the field, or bury them in the compost heap. Some slugs will burrow through potting compost, but the problem is not as bad as in the open ground. Hostas, for example, do much better in pots as our gastropod friends do not enjoy the feel of terracotta on their bellies. A mulch of coarse grit on the surface of the compost completes the obstacle course.

If a really persistent slug or snail has climbed up overnight, munched and gone away, it is worth brushing the sides of the pot with a stiff brush, then sweeping underneath and around it. With any luck, this will prevent the culprit and the rest of its family from following the slime trails back to the same plant the next night.

The dreaded vine weevil

Next on our 'Wanted, Dead' list are the evil weevils, whose larvae become more active as compost temperatures rise. We have tried soaking the rootballs of vulnerable plants in expensive and revolting insecticide – with limited success – and we are not keen on using compost that contains insecticide (as many nurseries do). Perhaps next year we will try applying nematode treatments.

Meanwhile, heucheras and echeverias seem to be our vine weevils' favourite meal, closely followed by London Pride, *Saxifraga* x *urbium*, and many lilies (notably *Lilium* Citronella Group). Plants that wilt suddenly, because vine weevils have attacked their roots, are

often salvageable as long as action is taken promptly. The crowns of heucheras can be split, washed carefully, trimmed and stripped of dying foliage, leaving shoots that can be grown on as cuttings to make decent plants by summer time. Echeverias can be treated similarly, as long as the weevil larvae has not bored right to the top of the rosette – it is essential to check that nothing is still lurking inside the trimmed stem that is to be replanted.

The compost from affected pots must not go in the garden or compost heap. We spread it thinly on the field or on a bare part of the vegetable patch for the birds to pick over. We grow a lot of lilies every year and re-pot them completely during the winter and early spring (before the adult weevils emerge to lay more eggs). This is expensive in terms of compost, but necessary to avoid a decimating plague.

The warmth of the greenhouse brings early crops of aphids, most of which are either squashed or removed wholesale on shoot tips pinched out between finger and thumb. Occasionally, we use a squirt of insecticide on a bad infestation but, on the whole, we tolerate a low-level population.

Yellow sticky traps are hung above the plants to catch whitefly (if you grow abutilons or regal pelargoniums you will have whitefly). Again, by dint of frequently picking off badly infested leaves, the population is kept to bearable levels, but never eradicated.

This year, Issy and Harriet are cursing because we have been raided by mice. Couscous the cat has not been earning his keep; whole pans of *Crocus vernus* ssp. *albiflorus* 'Pickwick', *Crocus tommasinianus* and the tiny *Tulipa linifolia* have been carefully excavated and mouse droppings litter the benches. The mice have chosen the smallest varieties, and we picture them scampering off with a little bulb in each cheek. Advice is taken and poison bait is put out. This does the trick, but too late for some of our spring plantings.

We always save some seed in summer and autumn from favourite plants, or ones that we just fancy trying – last year it was *Agapanthus campanulatus* and *Galtonia candicans*. This year we have *Salvia patens* 'Cambridge Blue' – will it come true? Little plants of yellow aquilegia and mauve *Semiaquilegia ecalcarata* are already lined up from last summer's sowings. A few plants of the semiaquilegia came from Hardy's Cottage Garden Plants in Hampshire, last year, and we liked it so much that we just had to try making more.

Growing from home-collected seed is deeply satisfying but, for our summer annuals, we buy new seed for quantity, reliability and vigour. There are always a few packets left over from last year, which may or may not work. Yet, the pleasures of winter and early spring include reading the seed catalogues and trawling local garden centres for interesting packets – and we are not above trying the freebies from gardening magazines.

As we peruse the brightly coloured envelopes, we keep this year's Chelsea theme in mind (white, silver, blues, purples). Impulse buys are allowed, as we are always looking for attention-grabbing oddities. We tend to over-buy as well, because growing from seed is always a gamble – the things may not come up, they may summon slugs from every corner of Warwickshire, or we may just not like them very much once they have grown. Spares can always be sold or given to staff if they cannot be shoe-horned in somewhere in the gardens.

There are certain regulars that we always grow. These include *Cosmos bipinnatus* for its billowing, feathery foliage and long-flowering series of crisp flowers in pinks and white, and *Calendula officinalis* – the proper orange pot marigold rather than the more tasteful shades that are now available. *Tagetes* (clear striped 'Jolly Jester' and the African marigold 'Vanilla' this year) and sweet pea, *Lathyrus odoratus*, are also obligatory. We like the old, richly fragrant varieties of sweet pea such as 'Cupani'.

In previous years we have grown a lot of the tobacco plants, *Nicotiana alata* and *N. sylvestris*, for their scent. This year, though, we are going to try to provide more of our Chelsea plants from seed, so there will not be room for the nicotianas' large, sticky leaves in the greenhouse.

Left: Seedpans were developed to save compost. These seedlings only need a couple of inches of compost to get them going, but will soon need pricking out into deeper pots.

When it comes to sowing, we find the addition of one part of perlite to three parts of general-purpose compost helps prevent seedlings becoming waterlogged and dying from either lack of air to their roots or damping off. We use shallow seed pans or square seed trays for most sowings, filled with about 5cm (2in) of soil. If the seeds are tiny, we mix them with dry sand to help us sprinkle them more evenly over the surface, and I keep a coarse sieve handy for a final thin covering of compost. I also have a very fine spray attachment for the hosepipe, as violent watering will either wash all the seeds to one corner of their pot or uproot tiny seedlings.

I sow bigger seeds, such as sweet peas or beans, in pairs in small longtoms, giving them a good 10cm (4in) of root depth. Then I pull out the weakest once the best is established. We start sowing in late February with climbers: *Cobaea scandens* (cup-and-saucer vine), sweet peas and Pink Olivers first. We now know that Pink Olivers are really called *Lophospermum erubescens* but, as this vigorous, pink-trumpeted twiner was given to Issy by someone called Oliver, Pink Olivers it shall remain.

To get the seed to germinate, we put the pots in the same propagator that we were using in autumn for the cuttings that are now all potted up and on the benches. Until we see them sprout, we also cover each pot with a sheet of glass to be absolutely sure that the compost stays damp. This, together with the heat below them, will get most seeds greening within a week.

Unless we are desperate to bring on the next batch, we leave the small seeds in the propagator until they are big enough to be pricked out, usually when they are about 5cm (2in) tall. This is a long job, sat at a bench between the radio and the heater. Each tiny plant is teased out from its fellows – I use an old pencil or ice-lolly stick to help. They are then spaced out every 5cm (2in) in another seed pan, pushed gently into the compost which, this time, is full to the brim, so giving about 7.5–10cm (3–4in) of root depth.

During the next few weeks we sow batches of *Antirrhinum majus*, *Cleome hassleriana*, nemesia, helipterum, *Senecio cineraria*, *Anagallis monellii*, brachyscome, salpiglossis and *Lobelia erinus*. Batch by batch, the seeds sprout and come out of the propagator, and batch by batch they are pricked out until, suddenly, the greenhouse is full and we must wait until it is warm enough to start using the polytunnel.

Tunnel of doom

This spring, the polytunnel has been a sad sight, as the March gales shredded the elderly polythene. We replaced the cover but the polytunnel is draughty and treacherous compared with the heated greenhouse. It does give some limited protection, however, and becomes useful as the worst weather recedes. As April begins and spring cuttings are taken and the small seedlings potted on, we run out of space in the greenhouse. Then hard decisions have to be made, and the hardier and older plants are put out to take their chances in the tunnel of doom.

Even more pressure is put on greenhouse space as the latest green babies are joined by trays of plug plants from Evesham nurseries – all of which need prompt potting on. Expense aside, plugs are a good way of obtaining a vast array of tender bedding plants. However, given the tiny amount of compost each one arrives in, it is imperative that they are transferred quickly to seed pans or individual 7.5cm (3in) pots, or they quickly starve to death.

Luckily, the greenhouse environment is much easier to manipulate than the polytunnel, with a thermostatically controlled gas heater, ventilators and even a small amount of supplementary lighting to hurry things along. By now it is a matter of watching to see what will be ready for our earliest summer displays, those going to Chelsea. If the helipterum is peaking too soon we move it to the shady end; no sign of flower on the verbena, so we put the plants under the light for a few days.

Last week, Issy and Harriet took time off from greenhouse duties, and went on an expedition in the pottery van, rattling off with the back full of empty crates. They were on their way to visit local nurseries and friendly head gardeners, and returned with a few exciting specimen plants which will give our new plantings the feel of maturity and fill the gaps we failed to plug ourselves. Most highly prized are the horticultural oddities that we know will have our visitors to the Chelsea stand exclaiming 'Ooh! What's that?' Our favourite and most generous source is Sue Dickinson, the head gardener at Eythrope.

What would your perfect garden look like? Perhaps, like me, you would be unable to choose between soft romanticism and the raked gravel of a formal parterre, but one contender must surely be the Victorian kitchen garden. Take its high red brick surrounding wall, gravely measured by immaculately fanned fruit trees, its large squares of vegetable garden, each with its own productive crops, the rows of sunken greenhouses behind sharp-edged yew hedges – what productive order! If you were to imagine all this kept with love and flair and skill, and add to it bright flower borders, fountains, corners of quiet lawn, and an orchard with pecking hens, you can begin to imagine the working garden at Eythrope and the atmosphere created.

The cherry house

This level of gardening is not possible for most of us – there are nine gardeners at Eythrope – but every time that I visit the gardens there, I leave uplifted and inspired, exactly as if I had been to a good art gallery. One of the many greenhouses at Eythrope is the Cherry House, for which, in 1991, we made 22 big pots. It is also, as far as I know, the only place in the country, perhaps even the world, where cherries are grown in this way, using knowledge that was inherited by Sue from the former head gardener, and he from his predecessor.

Every year, on February 14th, St Valentines Day, the cherry trees are carried inside the Cherry House by a team of five gardeners and placed on the freshly raked gravel, amongst the fan-trained peaches and nectarines which are grown in the borders along the inside edge of the house.

There is a feeding collar around the top of each cherry tree pot that is replaced each year, made from equal parts straw-rich manure and loam, mixed with water to the consistency of a mud pie. This is modelled by hand into a 7.5cm (3in) high collar around the perimeter of the pot. The tree will quickly put a web of feeding roots into this new collar. During February and March, the greenhouse is shut up at night, and on sunny days the floor and the trees are damped over, creating the right atmosphere to discourage pests (red spider and blackfly). When the flowers begin to open in late March, no damping down is done in the morning, so that the pollen is dry and ready for hand pollination at noon, which is done using a rabbit's tail tied to a stick. After this, the floor is damped again, in order to give the best conditions for the effective fertilisation of the flowers.

It will take several weeks for all the different varieties grown to complete flowering. Once set, the fruit must 'stone', a critical stage. The Cherry House must now be kept cool, so the ventilators and doors are left open day and night, as long as it is not too windy. The pots are watered once a week with lime water until the cherries have stoned: if successful, the fruit will be green, plump and shiny; if not, it turns yellow, shrivels and falls.

Facing page: The Cherry House of Eythrope with its 22 cherry trees in full blossom, each one grown in a 27in Whichford pot. Because they are flowering under glass, too early for the bees, each blossom must be hand pollinated every day using, in time-honoured fashion, a rabbit's tail on a stick.

Stoning successfully completed, water and food become paramount. Watering is helped by the reservoir formed by the feeding collar – uneven watering may cause the fruit to split. The trees are fed once a week with a high-potash fertiliser and damped over two or three times a day when sunny.

All new shoots on the trees are pruned back to three or four buds to encourage the formation of fruit buds for next year, discourage

Above: This freshly made feeding collar of manure and loam will both supply nutrients and act as a reservoir during watering.
Facing page: These cherry trees are looked after with such meticulous care that some are over 20 years old.

blackfly and to keep the trees a compact size. The blackfly can ruin the crop, so if cultural methods fail and blackfly persist, the house is fumigated organically.

Harvesting, the reward of so much intricate labour, is between May and mid-July. The varieties are 'Gloire de Heidelfinken', 'Van', 'Early Rivers', 'Merton Glory' and 'Bigarreau Napoleon' producing black, red and white cherries. Blackbirds are the pest at this moment, and they are kept out by mesh on the doors and ventilators. Fruiting finished, the trees are then stood outside for the rest of the summer. Some are twenty years old and are only replaced when they die in service. After a winter wash in January, the cycle starts again.

Theatre of auriculas

Eythrope also has a large collection of *Primula auricula* grown in specially made Whichford pots. The auriculas are grown as a single rosette in 7.5cm (3in) pots, with one flower stem, as if intended for show. A few 10cm (4in) pots enable some larger plants to be grown, and all are destined for the Auricula Theatre in a north-east corner of the vegetable garden, where they are displayed when flowering (see page 102).

The Auricula House, where the plants spend the rest of the year, is a north facing greenhouse with plenty of top and side ventilation, benches covered with gravel and a floor of Welsh slate. The house is shaded with blinds from March to September. The compost used is equal parts John Innes No. 2, peat and grit. Growth starts in late February, when they begin to be fed weekly with a high-potash feed until flowering finishes in May.

The auricula plants are repotted annually in July, dividing and removing as much old compost as possible. This is also an opportunity to check for vine weevil and root aphid. During September a high-nitrogen feed is given and in the winter the house is well ventilated and watering minimal.

Auriculas are one of a select group of flowers that caught the imagination of Western Europe in the early days of modern gardening. Believed to have first appeared in Europe around the mid-16th century, they were probably developed from crossing the yellow *Primula auricula* of Europe's mountains with other species of the genus *Primula*.

They became a particular favourite in England from the late 18th century, especially in the northern parts of the country and the Midlands. Here, Florist Societies were formed, mainly by working men. 'Florists' were enthusiasts who grew a limited range of flowers according to their society's strict code of rules. Other favourites included gold-laced polyanthus, carnations, laced pinks, ranunculus, double hollyhocks and old English tulips.

To the florists, judging was all-important. It usually took place in that other most English of institutions, the pub, where each plant was handed round those present and hotly discussed. The prize was often a copper kettle, which would have first been hung outside the pub to advertise the competition.

Show auriculas are not to be confused with their humble garden border cousins. They are altogether more delicate and require year-round care. In particular, they do not appreciate rain as this can damage the flowers, so they have to be kept in a greenhouse and watered without wetting the plant itself.

Be it show auriculas, cherries or our Chelsea plantings, greenhouses and flowerpots have always gone hand in hand. This is the way gardeners have kept an eye on their prize specimens ever since the early plant hunters of the 17th century potted up their 'exotic greens' and converted orangeries into greenhouses.

Above: Show auriculas must be protected from the rain throughout the year in an unheated greenhouse which is kept cool in the summer.
Facing page: The Eythrope auricula collection is put on annual show in its own theatre.

a host of bulbs

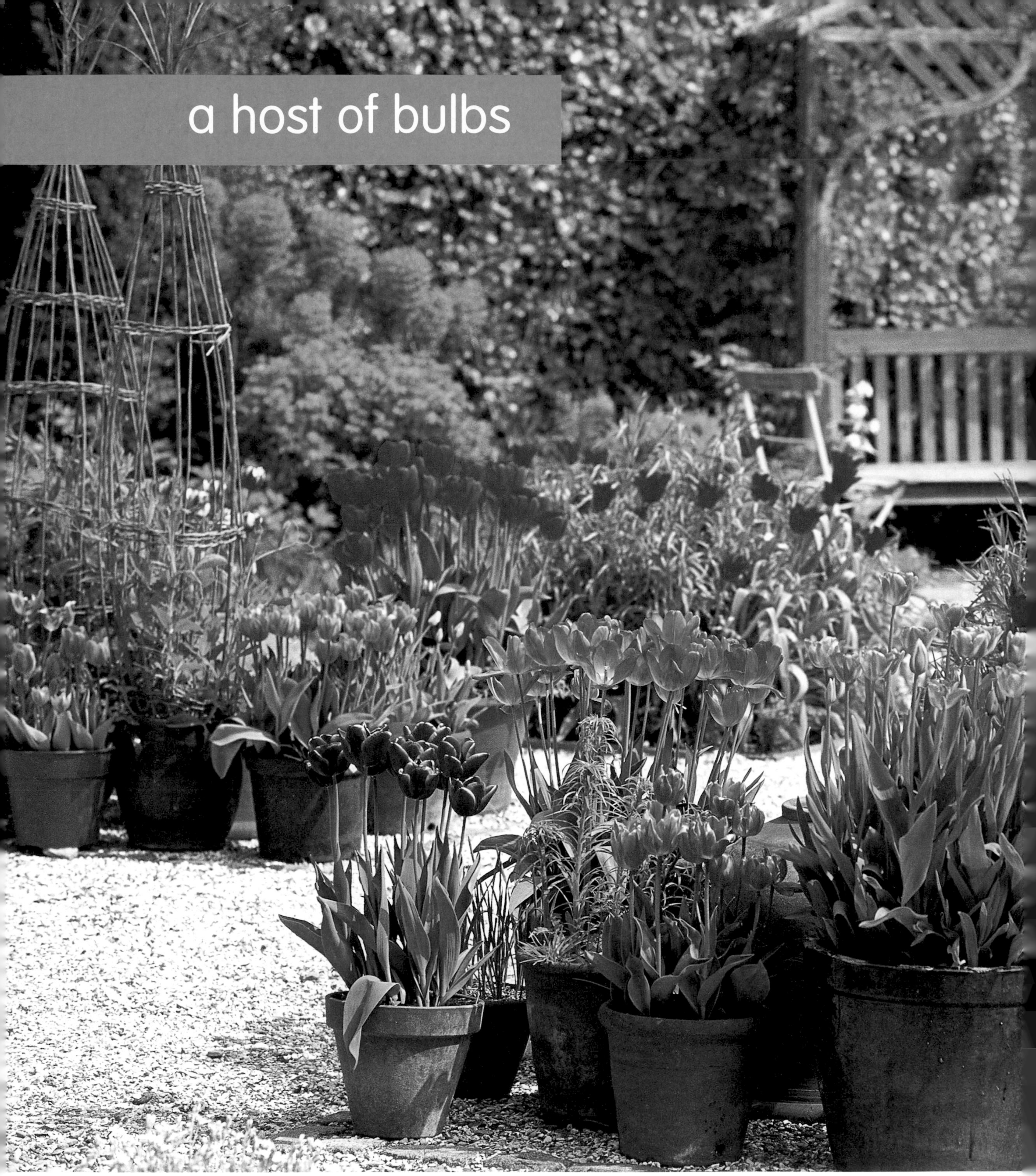

Luckily, back in the Whichford greenhouse, there are plenty of pots that have been spared the ravages of the bugs, slugs and mice, and as the weeks pass we begin to see whether the bulbs we chose in autumn have worked together. The mice bit the shoots off new crocuses planted in the flower beds but failed to find the hundreds of *Crocus vernus* ssp. *albiflorus* 'Pickwick' planted around a *Phormium tenax* in the huge Lizard pot. These shoots are fat and promising and soon open to wonderfully extravagant purple-striped blooms. Meanwhile, the mixed parrot tulips planted underneath them have started to push their leaves through the surface of the compost. In a few weeks, no-one will notice the dying crocus foliage beneath the riot of their crazily twisted and fringed flowers.

A rather smart snowdrop is *Galanthus nivalis* 'Viridapicis'. Despite having been planted as dry bulbs (always divide and replant snowdrops immediately after flowering if you can), it is an early star performer that sparkles in mixed plantings, but is also lovely as a simple clump in a green-glazed pot. The season's crescendo of yellow is led by the perky little *Narcissus* 'Jack Snipe'. The small narcissi are a reliable bridge from winter to spring, brightening up evergreen plantings and staying long enough to welcome the arrival of the big tulips.

The little pale, multi-headed *N.* 'Minnow' looks good with almost anything; *N.* 'Cheerfulness', with small double flowers, tones beautifully with yellow *Tulipa* 'Fringed Elegance' and *N.* 'Jetfire', with its orange trumpets and swept-back petals, wakes up any combination. We also welcome back old friends, planted in past years as novelties to us but now familiar. There's *N. bulbocodium*, for instance, which spreads its hoop petticoats beneath a clipped box, while *N.* 'Rip van Winkle' nods its shaggy head under a variegated holly.

Left: Be bold with bulbs! Blocks of bracing colour last for only a few days, but if you plan well, they will soon be replaced by later-flowering rivals, so the show can last right through to the summer.

For us, it is the jangling colours of the tulips that best celebrate spring. First, the few surviving *Tulipa linifolia* obligingly display their red flowers in little pans and baskets, and *T.* 'Mary Ann' shoots out surprisingly large flowers on their short stocky stems.

Then the fun really starts: *T.* 'Carnaval de Nice' pokes up promising foliage with pinky-white margins, before revealing its extravagant red-and-white striped and streaked flowers. The bright generous purples and blacks of *T.* 'Negrita', followed by *T.* 'Queen of Night', give new life to a pot of heucheras and purple and yellow violas, and allow pink *T.* 'Angelique' to sing. The names alone evoke prima donnas and princesses, and these ladies in their sumptuous taffeta ball gowns vie for attention. Flourishing today, we have the aristocratic 'Princesse Charmante' (in red) and 'Orange Princess', whilst previous episodes have featured 'Marilyn', 'Shirley', 'Maureen', 'Ballerina' and 'Beauty of Apeldoorn'.

Supporting roles

The supporting cast is more discreetly clad, but turns in accomplished performances. This year, we have tried some of the more unusual fritillaries. *Fritillaria persica* wins the Oscar for scene-stealing by extending a ladder of glaucous leaves high above violas and heucheras, where it displays nodding, deep purple flowers. Like all stars, it is expensive and has a reputation for being difficult – so we will wait and see if it earns its keep on a long-term basis. *F. michailovskyi* turns up wearing less elegant cloches of brownish purple edged in yellow, but provides middle-height interest and looks a more reliable sort.

Grape hyacinths are often shunned because we are contemptuously familiar with the rampant one, *Muscari armeniacum*. This is a tough bulb, which can work well contained in a pot, but it has cousins who are better behaved and more interesting. This year, we have *M. latifolium*, the flowers of which are at first neatly hooded by one of its leaves, allowing just a glimpse of the intense blue that eventually breaks out from its covering and shows off in several shades. We display them in an assortment of small pots on window-sills, near to eye level to allow closer inspection.

Another of this year's successes turns out to be *M. azureum*, with bright flowers lacking any hint of the purple that becomes a bit commonplace at this time of year. Last year, we had *M. comosum* 'Plumosum' which was, frankly, barmy. It arrived late for the party in a frizzy purple wig, just as the pot it was in had been moved away to allow the exhausted narcissi and tulips to die down gracefully, out of sight.

A major advantage of growing bulbs in pots is the ability it gives you to move them around – bringing them to a prominent position as they peak and moving them away when they start to go brown and flop. The flowering seasons of narcissi, tulips and lilies can be maximised by keeping them well watered but in a sunny position until their flowers begin to open. Then, they can be moved to a more shady, cooler site. Such rearrangements also give you the chance to try out more daring colour combinations. If you find the purple next to your orange makes your teeth hurt, then you can hastily separate the offending plantings.

Facing page: Tulip combinations are almost endless: here are four of Whichford's from this year. Top left: Red and blue in cream: the earliest tulip *Tulipa* 'Red Riding Hood' with *Muscari armeniacum* in an oval planter with shell handles. Top right: Red on red: *Tulipa* 'Maytime' with red daisies. Bottom left: Orange and blue pot with orange and blue flowers: kept against a shady wall, these parrot tulips *T.* 'Orange Favourite' lasted nearly four weeks. Bottom right: Gloss green, candyfloss and blue: a glazed pot embossed with a tulip shows off *T.* 'Carnaval de Nice'.

One of the most enthusiastic users of spring bulbs that I know is Kathy Brown and, last week, I went to visit her home at Stevington, near Bedford.

Just off the main road, Stevington is vaguely reminiscent of the Cotswold villages near Whichford, with the same russety golden ironstone used in the old houses. The great Bedford clay deposits are so near, however, that there is more brick mixed in, and the houses seem lower, more bunched up. In the middle of the village, at the crossroads squeezed between old houses, stands a fine medieval cross. Down the bank beyond I find Kathy's house, set in its beautiful gardens.

I have known Kathy for a number of years, from when she was researching and writing her book about container gardening, after her PhD research into the finances of 18th-century country estates. In 1982, after she had given up her job at the Bank of England to bring up her children, she was casting around for a part-time job, Kathy and a friend lit upon the idea of door to door plant selling in her area of north London. Having been brought up on a farm in Shropshire, perhaps this was the nearest green antidote to city life.

While husbands were left weekend baby-minding, Kathy and her friend at first sold bulbs in October, and fuchsias, geraniums and so forth in early summer. Soon, however, they were being asked for ready-planted containers, and in particular terracotta.

As a teenager, Kathy had often gone with her mother to the local flower arranging club, the first hint in the rural Shropshire of the 1960s that there were other possibilities for women's talent beyond mundane domesticity. Kathy now treated her clients to

longer-lasting displays, using those flower arrangers' ideas of structure and colour.

Having already published one book during her former career as a banker – on the history of Hambro's – she soon decided to do the same in her new field. Kathy has always relished research, and history plays a serious part in her books. You can see the influence of Victorian colour schemes in her plantings, especially those of John Mollison. A number of his plant recipes, found in his 1879 *The New Practical Window Gardener*, she has recreated to great effect around her own house which, coincidentally, dates from 1876.

Pink and white, bright blue and red with a dash of yellow, all were thrust together in an unselfconscious riot of colour. How different from the genteel refinement of Vita Sackville-West's White Garden at Sissinghurst of a generation later. The world of these plantings was confident and brash, as yet untainted by the introspective doubt heralded by Freud. In the 20th century, this style survived in parks departments and a few suburban gardens. But smart gardens became more sophisticated and harmonious and eschewed such jangling clashes of colour.

Kathy is firm in her belief that gardening is an art, and likes to take inspiration from painters. As I arrived, I was assailed in the quiet grey of the Bedfordshire countryside by a giant slab of the artist Mondrian: precise blocks of colour painted on to a badly placed pre-existing concrete wall by her son. In front, bold stands of tulips in shiny blue Vietnamese pots announce a garden full of colour.

Kathy's collection of terracotta flowerpots is eclectic. It includes old orchid pots, their many holes seeming to suit the tree ferns planted in them, as well as several generations of Whichford pots. There are Mexican pots carved with iguanas and crocodiles, and small pots delicately painted with motifs of zebra or lizards darting through a haze of dots, painted by an ex-Wedgwood artist.

Facing page: The shock of primary colours in both Mondrian-style background, pot and yellow tulips (top right) is a theme that carries on in the nearby disused swimming pool (below). Kathy Brown's spring garden can also, however, be found in gentler moods, as with this spring bouquet of polyanthus and narcissi (top left).

Although I was visiting Kathy primarily to admire her displays of spring bulbs, I also wanted to see how her permanent plantings were faring. Being in sole charge of her hundred or so pots, she insists that most of her creations should not only be low maintenance, but also last for several years before needing replanting. It's the opposite balance from those at Whichford, where we have a few permanent favourites, but most plantings will be dismantled every couple of seasons.

She makes much use of hostas, Tasmanian tree ferns and native British ferns and, at this time of year, hellebores underplanted with *Iris reticulata* varieties and white heathers, or snowdrops and aconites. The bulbs are often in their second or third year, like the tiny daffodils pushing up through thick gravel beside a variegated London Pride.

At Whichford we do something similar with our alpine gardens. Ever since I was a boy I have been fascinated by landscapes in miniature, and alpines lend themselves to this idea. We fill as large a shallow pan as we have with a compost mixed with plenty of added sharp sand for drainage. Then we create rock outcrops from tufa or any interesting-looking stones, cramming in a good variety of plants around them. Bare earth is covered with gravel or slate, replicating the scree mountainside where many alpines originate. Pot culture seems to suit alpines well and, in spring, their delicate flowers create a tiny universe all of their own.

Kathy also has a fine collection of succulents that she overwinters in a heated dome greenhouse. Aeonium, eucomis, *Agave filifera*, *Echeveria elegans* and the spiders' webs of *Sempervivum arachnoideum*, each allowed over the years to colonise, clump or trail down according to their nature. This long-term approach leads to an effect that is unmannered, uneven and reminiscent of how plants would grow in their natural habitat.

I reflect on this as I survey the array of plants in our greenhouse. We, too, have aeoniums, magnificent specimens given to us by Sue Dickinson. However, we will use them with plants from many different natural habitats, and in plantings designed to look their best from now until the autumn frosts, when they will have to be reworked.

Left: Alpines grow well in pots, which mimic their natural habitat, although here rock outcrops are replaced by the chasms and cliffs of our terracotta pots. Facing page: A giant seedpan (we nicknamed it a widebottom) is generous enough to take a whole landscape in miniature, with mossy rocks, gnarled logs and spring-flowering alpines creating their own microcosm.

chelsea planting scheme

Today we are going to finalise the Chelsea plantings. In the past, we have often 'bodge-planted' Chelsea displays on site, transporting the plants and pots separately and planting under a thin layer of compost without removing the plants from their plastic pots. This is the usual practice for Show Gardens. This year, though, we want to plant up the pots properly at Whichford, so that the plantings will have a few days to knit together before being shipped off to the show. We have got one panel of the backdrop ready, resplendent with its glowing red fresco, propped up against one of the greenhouse benches.

Now is the moment of reckoning, when we test whether or not the plants that we have collected really will work together and gleam against the red as planned.

Our palette is light to contrast with the tonally dark background – any other colour would look dingy against this. Plants have been chosen for their soft green foliage, avoiding any dark leaves. White will obviously feature heavily for flowers, with pale blue bridging the gap between that and the grey. Dusky pink and purple will lead the eye back to the dark red walls, and we have a few shocks of pink and orange waiting in the wings if we decide we need some wake-up focus.

We have also been careful to choose pots that suit this environment. It may be a small space, but the Roman arch that defines its far side is 3.6m (12ft) tall – a grand piece of architecture. It is large enough to be flanked by two enormous urns that we have made especially. To finish this backdrop with a suitable Italianate flourish, we have a pair of 4.5m (15ft) olive trees which we will under-plant with silver thyme, an assortment of sempervivums and some *Allium karataviense*, all amongst tufa and gravel. With these as anchors, I plan to work forwards either side of the central pathway in two parallel rows. I will have pairs of almost identical plantings gradually shifting from silver and white through our greys, blues and purples. Ending at the front of the garden will be a few more intense reddish and blackish purples, with silver foliage threading all the way through.

Facing page: These plantings steer clear of strong greens, preferring grey, silver and even blue foliage (right), while purple oddities provide interest, especially the *Aeonium* 'Arnold Schwarzkopff' (left).

Below: *Tradescantia pallida* 'Purpurea' is also a good focal point (right). Otherwise, the flower colour is almost entirely white, with occasional blushes of pink or purple (left).

At Whichford we are habitually close planters. We like our displays and flowerbeds to overflow with plants pushing through each other. For Chelsea, this effect needs to be achieved almost immediately at a time when most plants are only just getting going. So we always stuff them in, ignoring textbook strictures about planting distances and respect for fragile rootballs. The large pots we have selected for Chelsea swallow a great many plants.

Although we have our plan as a guide, the success of the final display depends on a lot of trial and error. The neat and tidy greenhouse, already crammed with plants, soon grows chaotic as plants are brought in or passed forward for assessment – to be debated over, accepted and propped up in a pot, or rejected and plonked back on the bench. Once the plant combination for a pot is chosen, the pot is planted up properly, and so is its pair. After a while, we can only move around the greenhouse sideways, holding our breath, trying not to break soon-to-flower shoots.

In front of the giant pots and their olive trees, we decide on a pair of large orange pots, simple 83cm (33in) pots with a single decorative band. In each one are three cardoons, *Cynara cardunculus*, with their spectacular arching silver leaves providing the tall centre. Round this group are several osteospermums, including *O.* 'Silver Sparkler', which has variegated foliage and white flowers with purplish blue backs to the petals. There's *O.* 'Whirligig' too, whose flowers, also in white and purple, are so good with their quirky pinched starburst petals that we disregard the stronger green of their foliage.

As for the rest of the scheme, *Argyranthemum* 'Qinta White' provides height and plenty of spidery double white flowers. *Helipterum roseum* 'Pierrot' is also selected for bright white flowers on tall stalks with discreet, glaucous foliage. The variegated foliage of *Pelargonium* 'Lady Plymouth' and trailing nepeta are blended in

around these, keeping the overall effect against the red fresco background in mind. The variegation must be whitish not yellow so that the more silvery foliage is not dulled. *Pelargonium crispum* 'Variegatum' is rejected for this reason.

We try heucheras and pink verbenas, but they look too dark and blobby for the far end of the garden. *Diascia* 'Snowdrift', on the other hand, works well. Just a couple of plants provide sprays that thread through the whole planting, completing the frothy effect.

That was a good start. We work on, grabbing plants, rejecting them, trying them again with something else, blending foliage: the silvery leaf of *Convolvulus cneorum* has to be matched carefully, and we decide that *Senecio cineraria* 'Silver Dust' will do while the *Helichrysum petiolare* is definitely too yellow next to it. We wish we had *Cerinthe major* 'Purpurascens', with its intense blue-purple bracts, but there are only a couple of leggy plants that have self-seeded in the greenhouse benching.

Key plants include *Sedum alboroseum* 'Frosty Morn' and the Japanese painted fern *Athyrium niponicum* var. *pictum*. We soon begin to run out of the latter and Harriet goes to dig some out of my garden, where they had been released after last year's Chelsea.

Facing page: To think of new plant combinations (or perhaps to say discover them would better convey the excitement) you have to break away from the usual. Ruby chard we normally grow in the vegetable garden, but as it is frost hardy we have tried it here to great effect with little *Muscari armeniacum*. The pot is interesting, too. A press-moulded pot, it is decorated with our Whichford roulette when it is leather hard and then painted with colour. This coating is then scraped off the surface leaving the lettering inlaid with colour.

Eye-catchers

As we move forward in the plan, we allow ourselves to include something a little bolder and brighter to catch the eye of Chelsea visitors caught in the current that sweeps down the main avenue. A pair of seraphim pots will be raised up at eye level against the side walls, where their ornate late Renaissance Dutch handles and cherubim faces will be seen to best advantage. We choose the strong, fleshy tresses of the iridescent *Tradescantia pallida* 'Purpurea' to drape over their rims, and risk the abrupt contrast with blue-grey echeverias and the peculiarly blue-leaved *Argyranthemum foeniculaceum* 'Royal Haze'.

In a pair of large basketweave pots beneath these seraphim pots, we include bright white *Pelargonium* 'Arctic Star' with its odd, jagged leaves. As we are nearing the front of the garden, we put in the strong blackcurranty pinks of *Verbena* 'Tapien Pink' and the *P.* 'Barbe Bleu'. Reliable *Salvia officinalis* 'Purpurascens' ties the greys and pinks together. We might have used the sumptuous regal pelargonium *P.* 'Lord Bute' here (we have some lovely specimens), but it has too much leaf weight for each flower.

In a moment of madness, intense orange-red nasturtiums nearly get in, but discipline prevails. Nine times out of ten we would use such a colour to wake things up a bit, but this time we want the plantings to be suitably elegant for their classical setting, so avoid a clash that might lower the tone.

Right at the front of the garden, we need a star performer. The path coming from under the Roman arch widens from 1.8m (6ft) to 2.4m (8ft) as it comes forward, with the beds of pots to either side. This extra width at the front allows for a pot to stand full in the centre of the path, splitting the entrance in two. We have chosen our emblem to go there, the Ham House urn. The heavy swags and gadroons on the bowl are taken from gate finials at Ham House, in Surrey, and make for an impressive pedestal urn.

Facing page: You need an ebullient centrepiece to catch the eye at Chelsea. One year we went sub-tropical, planting up this (1m) 39in baroque urn with tree fern, cordyline, phorminum, crotons and the exotic flowers of *Strelitzia reginae*.

Star of the show

What we need in it is a plant that will catch the eye of plant enthusiasts. Finally we have found a home for Sue's enormous, almost black *Aeonium* 'Zwartkop'. We underplant it with *Convolvulus cneorum* and get enthusiastic about the contrast between the dark purple-black rosettes and its silvery leaves and white, crumpled flowers. A couple of Japanese painted ferns, *Arthyrium niponicum* var. *pictum*, to share the colours of both partners, and we are finished.

It is an exciting moment when you realise that your paper scheme actually works. Months of plant collecting and growing come to fruition – not quite what I imagined, as every plant has its own shape and variations of colour that always leads me to changes on the day, helping to suggest a particular character for each planting.

Tomorrow we will finalise everything, and soon it will be time to get ready for the move to Chelsea. We will pack crates with small pots filled with intriguing succulents, spare plants and pots, string, scissors, trowels and hose fittings. Then everything will have to be loaded on to the articulated lorry, already half-full with the enormous olive trees that we are using. All our fragile plantings, loosely wrapped in cling film or horticultural fleece, will be wedged in among the horizontal olives. There will be many muttered prayers that the lorry does not lose them on a sharp corner on the way to London.

While we have been working, the wind has freshened and blown up some ragged clouds from the west. It looks as though we are in for a spate of April showers in early May. I shall take my chances of getting a soaking and take the dogs for a walk in the woods, where the bluebells are just beginning to lay out their fragrant carpet underneath the hazel and oaks.

We check the vents and the heating settings, and shut up the greenhouse doors – this is no time for a lapse in concentration! Outside, the birds sense the changing air and vie to out-sing each other in a glorious cacophony, joyfully marking out their stretches of the freshly greened hedge. The dogs jump up and wheel round me, tumbling over each other in snarling play. I pull on my coat as I walk into the gusting wind, lengthening my stride. All nature is alive and quickening about me.

From spring until the end of summer, make sure plants are watered regularly. In most cases, the soil should be moist but not waterlogged. Alpines and succulents will tolerate dry conditions and require less watering. Also, start feeding plants during the growing season – roughly once a week. Apply a liquid feed, or you can add slow-release granules to the compost when potting up. Some plants prefer a rich, more fertile, compost than others and this is indicated in the key.

Perennials

Asphodeline lutea **S; T; WD**

Dicentra spectabilis **PS–Sh; R**

Euphorbia griffithii 'Fireglow' or 'Dixter' **F; PS**
  (contact with sap of euphorbias may cause irritation)

E. myrsinites **F; PS**

E. polychroma **PS**

Lamium galeobdolon **F; Sh**

L. maculatum **F; Sh**

Primula auricula **PS–Sh; R; WD**

P. denticulata **PS–Sh; R; WD**

P. Gold-Laced Group **PS–Sh; R**

Pulmonaria eg 'Blue Ensign', 'Sissinghurst White'. **Sh; R**

Bulbs

Allium karataviense **F; S; T; WD**

Fritillaria imperialis **S; T; WD**
  (After flowering, fritillaries prefer a dry summer dormant period)

F. meleagris **S; WD**

F. michailovskyi **S; WD**

F. persica **S; T; WD**

Muscari armeniacum **S–PS**

M. azureum **S–PS; WD**

M. latifolium **S–PS; WD**

Narcissus – many varieties, including 'Thalia', 'Cheerfulness', and 'Minnow', (see also Winter list, page 80) **S–PS; WD**

Scilla sibirica **S–PS; WD**

Tulipa kaufmanniana **S–PS; WD**

T. greigii **S–PS; WD**

T. linifolia **S–PS; WD**

Plus many tulip varieties **S–PS; WD**

Alpines/miniatures

Antennaria var. *rosea* **S; WD**

Armeria maritima **S; WD**

Berberis x *stenophylla* 'Corallina Compacta' **S; WD**

Iberis sempervirens **S; WD**

Ipheion 'Rolf Fiedler' **S; WD**

Primula allionii **S–Sh;**

Ranunculus ficaria 'Brazen Hussy' **S–PS; R**

Saxifraga – many varieties **S–PS, WD**

Evergreen shrubs

Camellia japonica **E; Sh**

C. x *williamsii* **E; Sh**

Choisya ternata **P; S**

Pieris 'Forest Flame' **E; PS–Sh**

Deciduous shrubs

Berberis thunbergii 'Red Pillar' **F; S**

Crataegus monogyna **PS–Sh**

Biennials/bedding

Bellis perennis **S–Sh**

Erysimum cheiri **P; S**

Digitalis purpurea **S–Sh**

Myosotis hybrids **S–Sh**

Viola – (carrying on from winter) **PS–S**

Key

E:	Prefers ericaceous compost
F:	Interesting foliage
P:	Scented foliage or flowers
PS–Sh:	Thrives in partial shade or shade
R:	Likes a rich, fertile soil (add organic matter, such as leaf-mould)
S:	Prefers a sunny site
S–PS:	Will tolerate sun or partial shade
S–Sh	Happy with either sun or shade
Sh:	Thrives in a shady position
T:	Talking-point/attention-grabber – people will ask you what that plant is!
WD:	Requires a very well-drained soil that includes added grit or coarse sand.

Facing page: Pots take centre stage in spring, before summer borders have filled out and started to flower.

summer

It is still deliciously cool. I pad across the lawn, feeling the cut grass sharp under my bare feet. The old willow trees behind the pottery rustle in the early morning breeze and, stretching, I take in the sun through the kaleidoscope of their leaves. Beyond, in the orchard, feathery heads of the meadow grasses are heavy with seed.

The unpredictable English summer has given us a heatwave and it is about to turn into a drought. Where the lawn lifts over the ruins of a long-flattened haybarn, the grass is already brown and crisp. Today it is covered by a new carpet of yellow – to preserve water, the willows are shedding their leaves as if it were already autumn. And today is set to be another scorcher.

Too hot to handle
In this heat, life in the pottery becomes extreme. In winter, we bless the kilns for their warmth and, for that reason, the whole pottery is built around them. But now, in high summer, they make the pottery almost dangerously hot. Upstairs, the extractor fans are full on all day, the windows wide open to catch the slightest breeze, and we work in uncharacteristic silence, conserving energy like the willows. This heat is something to be endured.

In more leisurely eras, we could have avoided this roasting from the kilns. Nowadays, our customers expect us to respond very quickly to their orders, so we need regular firings to keep up. Our kilns are small compared to most traditional designs, which would have been filled far less frequently, keeping the customers waiting but allowing more harmony with the seasons.

At Wrecclesham, we fired a huge up-draught bottle kiln once every six weeks. It took three days to load, two to fire up and three to cool. At Les Rairies, in central France, they still have a system of kilns and drying sheds built in the 17th century. They split their year into two, making and drying pots in spring and summer, and firing kilns in winter when frost might destroy any still-wet ware.

Who would choose to stoke the fireboxes with wood day and night in this heat? If we are not careful, on a day like this the hot breezes will firm up the pots before the decorators have had time to embellish them, and if the pots dry too quickly they will crack as they shrink. Luckily, these days we have long lengths of thin plastic sheet to help us which we can drape over the drying pots to hold them back. Traditional potters would have only had damp sacking at their disposal.

I climb up the brick staircase that leads from my garden into the workshop. It is made from the remains of an ancient barn that, before the pottery was built 20 years ago, marked the edge of the village. Since then, it has transformed into a small arched loggia with a flat-roof terrace above. From here, you look back to the house and to the woods beyond the village, and the garden is laid out around you in the morning sun.

I walk across the terrace, lift the latch and go into the workshop. It stretches away in front of me, a line of wheels on the north side, the pots on their orderly racks to the south. The windows are covered by makeshift blinds to help protect the pots from the sun. I walk the length of the room and slide open the door that we keep shut to isolate the drying area directly above the kilns from the other workshops. Already the heat is rising up through the slatted floor – and the kilns are not even near top temperature yet. Through another sliding door, and I am in the other, newer, upstairs workshop, a large irregular shape, this time open to the roof trusses right up to the apex of the roof. This great volume of enclosed air seems to slow down drying, and makes the room ideal for the making of bigger pots.

Facing page: The full summer sun at Whichford: gazenias bursting with flower and glowing terracotta.

This morning I have come to check the pieces that I am to work on later. I hope to find them in that happy state, neither too soft nor too hard. This is doubly important today because I shall be using the pots in a very particular way, joining them together, one on top of another, to form one gigantic urn.

In the past, large pots were made for all sorts of applications – laundry tubs, for tanning, as storage tanks for oil, wine, or wheat, even crucibles and acid jars. The only use that has not been superseded by modern materials or technology is that of the

flowerpot – how could you imagine an Italian villa with its rows of orange trees in stainless-steel tubs?

There are a number of technical problems to overcome if you are to make large flowerpots. If you are throwing, which is the quickest way to form pots, height is limited to the length of the potter's arm, so anything taller than 46cm (18in) is problematic. Also, centring and throwing become dramatically more difficult and energy-consuming as the weight of clay increases. Half a hundredweight is about the limit. To solve this problem, different cultures have arrived at various ingenious solutions.

Below: Italian gardens have been full of citrus trees in big pots since the early Renaissance, a habit adopted from Islamic Sicily.

Above: Franco Massini hand-building in Impruneta. He is one of three brothers who work in the family business with their father, sharing an antique kiln with their uncle.

Above right: Finished pots stacked amongst the vines at the back of their pottery.

Imprunetan pots

In Italy, to make their beautiful vases they do not use throwing at all, nor even a turntable. Today, if you visit Impruneta, near Florence, you will notice lines of olive jars on display outside the old buildings, each one a subtle variation on its neighbour. On the shoulder of each is scratched or stamped the name of the maker and, next to this, the year. I have seen last year's jars standing next to their 18th-, 17th-, even 16th-century ancestors. They cannot properly be called copies, as they are part of an unbroken line of production stretching from the Renaissance. Many of the workshops used remain almost unaltered from those days, and the clay is from the same pits. Often it is also the same families that work them: a rare and precious survival for this day and age.

When you first venture inside an Impruneta workshop out of the glare of the summer sun, your eyes cannot make anything out, for these are dark, cool places. Whereas the pottery at Whichford is built to cope with long, wet and sometimes cold winters, here everything is designed to mitigate the torrid heat of summer. Natural light, which brings heat, is banished and the kilns are set at the far end of the building, as far away as possible from the making areas.

These days the enormous fireboxes of the kilns – 'wolf mouths' they are still called – are fed by oil as well as logs, with bundles of faggots reserved for the very end of the firing. The long flames that curl up from the faggots pull the heat that has built up in the fireboxes right up through the load.

The cupboard at the Massini pottery: old racks, sieves, frames and wine casks.

A coiled creation

The local clay here is grey and its colour gives everything in the workshops an extra dusting of antiquity. The present occupants are firmly marked in their time by baseball caps and T-shirts, but the methods they use belong to any time in a long past. After first beating out a pizza-shaped roundel, they take a handful of very soft clay and roll it between their hands into a long irregular coil, which they then place around the edge of the pizza, joining on new coils as required, ascending in a corkscrew fashion. All the time, they shuffle backwards around the pot which remains static on its work plinth, knitting new coils to those below with a deft squeeze and a twist of the wrist.

After four or five coils, the pot will be about 23 or 25cm (9 or 10in) high and the inside and outside will be smoothed off. The pot is then left to stiffen while another is worked on. Any more coils now would make the fresh creation buckle out of shape or collapse, but when it is harder, another series of coils can be added, left to dry, and so on until the pot has reached its full height.

Diameter and curve are calculated either by eye and experience or by lining up the growing pot with chalk outlines drawn on nearby walls. By the time the rim of a large olive jar is finally reached, the bottom of the pot will be almost dry. So any clay decoration is added as the pot progresses, because it must shrink at the same time and rate as its host, otherwise it may peel off.

The classic Italian orange pots are also produced in this way. Their rings and bands are finished off to the sound of rhythmically scuffling feet as the potter, intent on the finishing details, shuffles with back bent around the pot, smoothing, adjusting the exact curves of the mouldings with a scrap of wet chamois leather between his fingers. The round baubles of the Medici crest, or that of some other great family, may be added, but otherwise those pots remain simple.

Baroque times brought a taste for less austere pots and the potters obliged by adding a profusion of cornucopia spilling out long swags of fruit, pinned back by grinning satyrs, all set on a bed of acanthus or oak. Classical antiquity was ransacked for ideas but, with every new element added, the potters' job became harder – all those fiddly bits could fall off as they dried, or be knocked off in the kiln.

Never short of invention the potters of Impruneta changed how they worked to suit this new taste. They would make the decoration integral with the pot, so that it could never fall off: they would press-mould the whole pot.

Impressive press-moulds

As we have seen, press-moulding is a very ancient technique, but it was given new possibilities with the invention of plaster of Paris. It was invented in the 18th century using the gypsum deposits beneath Montmartre. This had been heavily exploited since the Royal Decree that all of Paris's old wooden buildings must be plaster rendered to help avoid a Parisian version of the catastrophic 1666 Fire of London. This new type of highly refined plaster

enabled larger moulds to be reliably made with an accurate record of fine detail. The craftsmen of Impruneta were soon devising an enormous array of florid designs using the new casting material, many of which are still in production.

At Impruneta the moulds are made in the manner that we used in the spring at Whichford to make our herm; a clay original, resplendent with all its detailed ornament, is cast in a suit of plaster. For round pots, however, it is usual to have four breaks quartering the encircling plaster vertically. These are held together during making by encircling straps tightened by tourniqués, or sometimes a special plaster ring that overlaps the top edges of the four vertical side pieces.

Part of a kiln load in Impruneta. In the foreground 'pavimenti' paving bricks (good kiln fillers), then plain conical pots, square boxes and a pair of traditional olive oil jars.

The Whichford mould

In 1985, we first made a similar 18th-century style pot at Whichford inspired by this system. For many years, it was the largest in our catalogue, measuring 98cm (39in) in diameter when fired.

In shape, it is a standard conical flowerpot, with a massy rim covered in a repeated oak-leaf pattern. Beneath this forest hang four garlands, heavy with the ripe fruit and flowers that spill from the mouths of cornucopia, the classical horn of plenty. These spring from behind the heads of grinning goat-horned satyrs, and from their beards dangle more bunches of fruit.

This activity is all in the upper part of the pot. Around the middle runs a twisted rope – I always imagine it as silken – a motif that is repeated around the base. In between these two bands, acanthus plants unfurl their spiky leaves. The overall effect given by this decoration is one of riotous plenty, hardly surprising when so many ancient symbols of fecundity, renewal and natural vigour are woven together in one design.

To achieve the 43cm (29in) of height required for this monster pot (it uses up over four hundredweight of clay in the making), the mould is not only broken into quarters vertically, but also divided into three layers horizontally, giving a total of 12 sections. These have to be carefully pieced together before each making. The largest sections need three people to manoeuvre them into place, and then to remove them again. It's a process that is done gradually over several days, starting from the top layer, so that the lower part of the pot remains supported the longest to prevent a collapse. When the rim is first liberated, it is also propped up on long, pad-ended sticks to help take the weight whilst the clay stiffens.

Much work has to be done to a press-moulded pot once it leaves its parent mould. In addition to the repairing and filling of blemishes left where the clay has not been sufficiently firmly beaten into a nose or an oak leaf, we also add many details, especially undercuts, which give our press-moulded pots their individual life.

Our biggest pot takes several days of patient labour to build up its full character, with Linda moving from favourite cushions to low stool and back again, as she tries to keep comfortable beneath her overhanging task, tools laid out beside her on the floor. When she

has finished, the pot will be wheeled away to a quiet corner and cosseted for three or four weeks – if it were allowed to dry any faster it would develop irreparable cracks and crevices.

Similarly, when it finally arrives in the kiln, the pot will have to be given kid–glove treatment, with an extra-slow and lengthy initial stage to allow any residual water from the inside of its thicker sections to steam away. Even though Linda will have cut up under the rim, it will still be 5cm (2in) thick in places, thick enough to harbour plenty of steam.

Facing page: This Baroque urn is made by beating clay into plaster of Paris moulds to give the basic form and decoration, which is then worked up for many hours by hand to bring the pot to individual life.
Above: The mould is built up in parts (the base section is pictured here), some of which need three people to manoeuvre them into place.

These storage jars were already old when the palace at Knossos in Crete was destroyed in about 1375BC. Similar pots have been made in Crete ever since, although they have now been transformed into flowerpots.

A third solution to the big pot problem combines the idea of coiling with the techniques of throwing. This is how Cretan potters made the jars that filled the labyrinths of King Minos, with their ridged decoration swirling around the jars as they lined the endless underground storage chambers of his palace at Knossos.

For 4,000 years, these types of jars have been made in Crete, once again used to hold olive oil, wine and laundry. In recent times, they have been adapted to satisfy our growing desire for flowerpots.

Since Crete is so near to where the wheel was invented, in Mesopotamia, it is reasonable to assume that this technique is a very ancient one. The pots produced today certainly have more than a passing resemblance to those which you can still see in situ in the labyrinth at Knossos (see left), and are made using clay from the same pits.

Cretan potters have adapted to the extremes of climate in their own way. They work only in the summer months. In the cold, wet winters they gather their pistachio and olive crops from the mountainsides for, like many craftsmen in the past, they are also farmers. The clay that they use is unusually tolerant of rapid drying, so they take no measures to protect the pots from the heat, as in Impruneta.

Instead, they work in the open air under sunshades made from rush matting. Their wheels are primitive – a simple shaft with a pointed fulcrum held by a wooden collar just below the wheel head. Motive power does not come from the thrower, but from his unfortunate assistant who squats beside the wheel and pulls at a stick passed horizontally through the main shaft, giving continuous, if jerky, motion. Initially, this is very hard work but, once the pot begins to grow, it acts as a kind of flywheel and helps to keep itself spinning evenly.

Aided by his assistant, each potter works on a line of up to ten wheels. He will know how many pots of each size he can finish in a day (the bigger, the fewer) and will work on that number of wheels. As in Impruneta, the pot is built up using thin coils added to a flat base, but now the wheel revolves past the static potter, allowing him to even out the coil by throwing.

One section completed, the next wheel is used until the whole line of wheels is filled. After a cup of Greek coffee, the ferocious summer heat will have dried the first-made pot sufficiently for those swirling, thumbed-on decorations to be squeezed, and then another coil can be added. This is repeated along the line of wheels, another coffee and another set of coils and so on, until the pots are finished.

Majorcan style

I found one final version in this repertoire of Mediterranean ways of making big pots, in Majorca. There, the base section is thrown on a wheel as normal – by starting with a large ball of clay – to the dimensions of the bottom half of the pot-to-be. The top section is then thrown neck down on a large round piece of wood (called a bat), with a diameter matching that of the lower half. After being allowed to stiffen slightly, the top is turned over, lined up and lowered onto the bottom half.

The bat is then cut off with a wire and removed. The whole pot is re-centred on the wheel and, after ensuring the join is good, the potter fills out the top half to its final, desired shape. We have used this technique at Whichford for over two decades to make all our ali baba jars and large flowerpots.

The two pots I am to make today are, however, far too big to throw in this way (in just two sections) and are even too big for us to press-mould – we would need a crane to shift the pieces of mould. Stimulated first by a private commission, and now by orders from Chelsea for those pots which held the olive trees, I have to construct pots over 110cm (44in) wide and 105cm (42in) high. They will eat up over a quarter of a ton of clay each, and it would be madness to try to centre such enormous lumps of clay.

The early morning light filters into the big making room beyond the kiln, creating shadows as I enter it. Along one side is a row of gently humming throwing wheels, each with a section of giant pot left slowly rotating overnight to ensure that they firm up evenly. I go over, stop the wheels and anxiously test each pot between finger and thumb. They seem about right, so I carefully cover each one in plastic and leave them, ready to work on. I go downstairs before I leave and adjust the big kiln; side bricks in, front burner on, back burner up a bit. It has been preheating overnight, and this earlier-than-usual routine will mean that the firing should be finished by late this afternoon and not need attention in the evening.

Cretan potters work outside all summer, returning to their pistachio and olive farms during the winter months. Here Dimitri is making a beehive pot in the traditional way.

If you don't need a base, why not, therefore, combine this upending with the Cretan technique of coiling and throwing? By using a small pugmill, we can extrude a much larger coil than those used in Crete – 10cm (4in) wide – on to the edge of whatever sized bat we need, centre it on a wheel and throw. All that pushing out from the middle is gone. In theory, simple. In practice, we have had to redesign the potter's wheel, ending up with a super powerful direct-drive electric one, capable of withstanding the enormous torques which we now generate at slow speeds without it stopping or blowing a fuse.

A joint endeavour

The pots will consist of four thrown sections, and the sections I have to make this morning are truly enormous. Simon and I struggle to lift what tomorrow will be the fourth and final stage onto the wheel on its 1.2m (4ft) diameter bat. We call for help and, when it is in place, each of us sits on a beer crate on either side of the turning coil. If I were to throw this myself, it would turn into a prolonged agony with my muscles kept at full stretch for too long to bear. I long harboured stories, almost myths, told me of Spanish potters working two, even three, on a wheel at once, and this is what we are now doing.

We place a tub of water on the slowly turning centre of the bat where we can both reach it, slap the coil rhythmically into shape, then start throwing. It seems far less than half the effort of working alone and it is strangely satisfying, even intimate, sharing the pot. A few words of consultation, or caution, as the work progresses, and it is done. The glistening, soft form is lifted off the wheel and replaced by the base section, thrown yesterday and now stiff enough to be built on.

Grasping the bat, Simon and I act as pivots as the second section is turned upside down by four of us, and we lift it gingerly on top of the base section. We wire off the bat and then throw the two sections, moulding them together as for any other two-piece pot.

Above: Three of us begin putting together a giant pot. The sections are thrown the day before by two of us together.

After breakfast, I return to the pottery. I am still nervous when it comes to making these giant pots. A large pot that does not work represents a huge amount of wasted energy and, if something goes wrong, they can be a very large slice of ugliness. Still, I have the excitement of a new experiment to help banish such fears. For, after 28 years of throwing, and with much help from the other potters, I have invented a new Whichford variant of those Mediterranean tricks for making big pots.

Using the Majorcan technique, we have made thousands of jars and large cone-shaped flowerpots. The top half, thrown, you will remember, at first upside down, doesn't actually need a base to it, the neck or rim being merely a ring of clay. Much effort is expended centring the ball of clay and then pushing it outwards from the middle to form a ring at the very outside of the bat. Only then can it be pulled up to form the needed cylinder. For 40lbs of clay, giving a 68cm (27in) rim, or even 60lbs, giving an 85cm (34in) rim, this is practical, but for uses beyond that it is enormously hard work.

By tea break, we have half-constructed the two enormous pots. They are left slowly spinning, their slight unevenness making the two of them perform some elegant, forgotten bourré as they sway to and fro.

For now, these pots must be left alone to stiffen, but in this summer heat I will return to them every two hours or so to check their progress. In winter, I would blast them with the full flame of a propane flame gun until they steamed, but such radical drying measures will today be performed naturally with a heat of almost Mediterranean brusqueness.

Outside, we sit around the walls of the raised flowerbeds and on the paving of the courtyard garden, tea and coffee and sandwiches spread about us. I see Issy's fingers absentmindedly reach out and nip off a faded flower – as summer gallops on, dead-heading becomes a habit. She has already spent an hour this morning with some tired-looking plantings, titivating, as she calls it, cutting out poor growth and picking off yellow leaves. Her constant attention to this satisfying task will keep our annuals and tender plants flowering from now right until the first frosts of late autumn.

Below: Four sections later, I sit beside the finished pot, relieved that it has all gone according to plan.

a changing climate

As I return to the house, I notice that the hornbeams, too, are dropping crispy leaves in desperation and that the robin is already singing his autumn song. What might we grow if global warming really were to tip us into a permanently hotter climate, I wonder? Perhaps one day the pottery will be clad in plumbago and bougainvillea, rather than clematis and honeysuckle.

Of course, our orange pots could be put to good use – how wonderful to gather oranges and lemons in the stockyard. But the old varieties of apples and pears in my orchard would not be so happy, and lotus thriving in the pond would definitely not make up for a lack of primroses in spring. We do now have those olive trees in pots and many people claim to overwinter them easily outside. However, we are not so sure about a Whichford winter with its combination of cold and damp. Perhaps we will be proved wrong and, in a few years time, we will be selling glazed jars filled with our own olive oil.

If summers were consistently longer and hotter, and winters milder, we would grow gigantic pelargoniums like the ones you see outside houses in the Channel Islands. Or if more rain comes with increased warmth, perhaps our tree ferns would feel more at home. Much as we would love to include oleander, hibiscus, bananas or *Gloriosa superba* 'Rothschildiana' in our outdoor plantings, I am not sure that we would exchange these for the challenges of the changing seasons at Whichford. Nor would we want to exchange them for the rediscovery each year of horticultural treasures that only appear when the time and temperature are right.

All plants that thrive in the heat:
Facing page: The downy leaves and pink-stemmed flowers of *Plectranthus argentatus* are set off by the ash grey of an eclipse pot.
This page, above: The back steps up to the loggia terrace and the pottery are flanked by an eclectic mix of old pots planted with aeoniums and the upright *Pelargonium crispum* 'Variegatium'.
This page, below: A purple-tipped bougainvillea looking vibrantly healthy in a 50cm (20in) pot. It will be cut back hard in the autumn.

containing roses

The last of the scent from *Rosa* 'Paul's Himalayan Musk', trained against the loggia, drifts around the garden, exuding the languid essence of summer. It has been a vintage year for roses, and we have plenty of them. Some are free-standing while others climb the walls, drape themselves winsomely over seats and arches and collapse around a tunnel. I have forgotten the names of many, but a few will not let you forget their identity, like *R.* 'Constance Spry', one of my favourites. She lurks behind the arched door into the Paradise garden, her fat, pink blooms like some overpowering auntie, always waiting to assault you with her strange, spicy scent.

Many of these roses started their life at Whichford as pot plants. Given plenty of water and food, and support if they are climbers, roses make surprisingly good subjects for container growing. I grow them in 38 or 46cm (15 or 18in) pots by themselves. Then I liberate them when they become pot-bound, giving myself a large specimen that will quickly become established in its final home.

Longer stays are best tried in bigger pots, or the roots can be allowed to grow down through the large drainage hole that we always put in the bottom of our pots (as long as the pot does not need to be moved). Roses do not enjoy sharing their space and they are one of the few species that we never underplant.

As summer progresses, the perennial plants in the Paradise garden perform in turn. By June, the alliums and *Thalictrum aquilegiifolium*, in shades of purple, are everywhere, frothing around the shell pink of *Rosa* 'Fru Dagmar Hastrup' and fighting the pale blue iris. Above them, the white wisteria twines around the roof of the gazebo, while the tall ceanothus, leaning out over the wall, dusts the pots in the stockyard beyond with the blue of its fallen flowers.

No garden can do without roses. They can be grown well in pots (facing page), although we tend to plant them out after several years once they become pot bound. Right: a glazed ali baba reflects roses, loggia and the summer day. Top right: A newly emerged small elephant hawkmoth found in the Paradise garden.

While I wait for my pots to dry, I help Issy try to repair our automatic irrigation system, which delivers water via drippers spiked into the compost of the pots. This rather ugly system of little black pipes is very efficient when it works, allowing the water to seep down into rootballs with minimal wastage. It is programmed to come on in the early evening to give maximum effect.

This year, however, we have had trouble getting it to function properly, partly due to the ravages of a young puppy, and watering has had to be done with a hose for much of the season. It takes a long time to deliver enough water to a large planting by hose, as such a high proportion of it runs out of the bottom or straight off the top if the pressure is too great (taking soluble nutrients and a layer of compost with it). Each time a pot is watered in this way the compost is compacted a little more, reducing the oxygen available to the plants' roots.

The dripper system takes much longer to deliver the water, so avoids these problems. It is also good for plants that should not be splashed with water to minimise fungal disease, such as our ornamental pumpkins and echeverias. Issy and I find a few small pots that have been overlooked and are very dry. We plunge these into a bucket of water for a good soak. Eventually, we find the problem – an overlooked broken pipe – and make the necessary repairs.

The compost we are using this year contains a slow-release fertiliser. However, as the summer wears on, we may need to give the pots the odd liquid feed because they are closely planted. So we watch out for tell-tale yellowing leaves and lack of vigour. We are careful not to give the plantings excessive extra fertiliser, as we find that overfeeding causes brittle, sappy growth which supports more aphids than flowers.

Facing page: One of a series of urns (top left) commissioned for Queen Mary's apartments at Hampton Court Palace, painted cobalt over a tin glaze in the Delft manner. It is a challenge to plant it in a modern way – here we have underplanted

Liquid feed is all too easy to waste when poured on to the surface of a pot and runs off to pollute ground water. Besides, an excessively high nutrient content in dry compost can actually draw water out of roots. We find that there is little point in feeding temporary plantings after mid-August, as new growth will not have time to form flowers before the first autumn frosts.

As we pass, I see that Issy has clipped the topiary. The box is (ideally) clipped twice, with the first cut in midsummer. Cut it too early in spring or too late in autumn and you risk a flush of new shoots scorched by frost. Our yew seems to be less fussy and we have been known to be clipping our last shapes as flurries of snow arrive. However, this year we have done that job already, so that we can enjoy the play of sunlight on the newly crisp shapes.

We also look at the greenhouses, if only for a moment in this heat. There are not many plants left roasting there by midsummer, and some of the benching and slabs have been removed to make way for tomatoes. We spray the hose around the greenhouse most evenings. This helps to cool the atmosphere and harass the whitefly – and the raised humidity levels also discourage red spider mite.

The few remaining potted plants have all been recently repotted into the next size up so that they get the chance to spread their roots through the compost before the winter and reduce the risk of rotting. They are plants that we want to keep to grow as bigger specimens or as stock plants for cuttings. Our favourite salvias need to be potted on in bigger jumps than most plants, as they have unreasonably vigorous roots and quickly become unhappy in small pots. A greenhouse job that can wait for a rainy day in late summer is the taking of tip cuttings from tender perennials, and stem cuttings from *Lobelia cardinalis* and the toad lily *Tricyrtis formosana*.

white begonias with variegated thymes, some solenostemon for colour and trailing *Nemophila maculata* 'Five Spot'. We grow our lilies in pots to keep away slugs and snails. With careful autumn repotting, they will flower for several seasons.

potted herbs and vegetables

Round the doorway to the greenhouse is a cluster of pots full of herbs, which we use both for eating and for decoration. Sage, thyme and rosemary are useful mixers all year, bay is handsome (but needs a sheltered corner in winter) and fennel provides elegant feathery foliage which combines well with many plants. Marjoram, chives, parsley – all grow happily in terracotta and, as Issy so delicately points out, it does mean that you can put them out of the reach of peeing cats and dogs!

For us, vegetables and fruit are less easy, as they require more frequent watering than we can really provide in order for them to crop well. As we have so many displays to keep going, we have to know our limits. However, we do grow some of the more colourful vegetables, such as purple French beans, which did very well in a large pot facing south-west. We often include rainbow chard in displays for the striking red, pink or yellow midribs of its leaves, while decorative purple or white cabbages are also useful in winter displays. Strawberries can also be enormously satisfying to grow in terracotta – raising the fruit out of the way of moulds and slugs helps a great deal.

Apples can be grown on dwarfing rootstocks, varieties of tiny tomatoes, stumpy carrots, compact beans – you name it – have been bred to satisfy the patio gardener. Yet, if you can provide well-fertilised compost and plenty of water, it is worth trying many of the ordinary varieties in large pots. This is especially so if you do not have the right soil in your garden to keep them happy, or you do not have the space to spare for a dedicated vegetable plot.

Below: Herbs for outside the back door: sage, thyme and a pot of basil.

Above: With regular watering and feeding plus a fresh top layer of compost every autumn, oranges and lemons can be kept in the same pots for many decades. These pots are 70cm (28in) wide, and will be brought inside for the winter.

The summer garden

Since it is nearly lunchtime, Issy and I cannot resist a small wander around to admire the plantings we brought back from Chelsea, and congratulate ourselves on our design flair. We will carry on with proper work when it is cooler. Our crystal trophy from the Royal Horticultural Society for Excellence of Presentation is sitting smugly on its shelf in the showroom. After returning slightly battered from their travels, the plantings have grown on well and continue to fill out and improve.

In the absence of their Roman arch, the two big olive trees and their enormous pots have taken up position in the middle distance, drawing your eye across the field between the car park and the pottery to a far gateway and the hills beyond. They are so big that they effortlessly dominate quite a large open space. The other main pots from Chelsea now flank the pathway leading to the pottery, more spread out on their plinths than before, but keeping the same colour progression of dark to light.

The Ham House Urn is still centre-stage; it's the pot you see framed by the arch of hedge at the far end of the path as you arrive at the pottery. The convolvulus planted in it is now only silver leaves and is still waiting for its second flush of white flowers. It is set in an asymmetrical border full to bursting with flowers. In the background, rosemary and lavender are threaded through with the tall spikes of *Chelone obliqua* and *Cleome spinosa*, as well as the ever-present self-sown *Linaria purpurea*, thrusting up unbidden in both its purple and pink forms. Around the edges, *Euphorbia myrsinites* and lady's mantle, *Alchemilla mollis*, jostle for position.

Earlier, in late May and early June, the fresh growth of herbaceous plants was less boisterous, but pristine and promising. Hardy geraniums pushed up satisfying mounds, the delphiniums were already shooting upwards and *Santolina virens*, *Foeniculum vulgare*, *Phuopsis stylosa* and *Achillea millefolium* interlocked their cushions of glowing greens, hiding the dead foliage of earlier stars, the crocuses and hyacinths. As the tide of fresh foliage rose it gave a setting for our new green-glazed ali baba pots, placed on plinths in the beds. Several were quickly sold – perhaps, this year, everyone is hungry for glossy greens.

bedding room

No border would be complete without some summer bedding to give extra colour and a little variation over the years and, at Whichford, we use many of the same plants for this job as for growing in our pots. Each year, the perennial plantings in the borders fill out a little more. Next autumn, we must lift and divide some of them as, this year, obvious gaps for the insertion of bedding were hard to see. We did find some spaces, however. By early summer, tulip and late narcissus foliage always dies off rapidly and, although the violas and wallflowers were still producing some very attractive flowers, we ripped them out.

During the weeks running up to Chelsea, plants destined for bedding out, rather than showing, are sometimes sorely neglected. When we were short of time, they were not potted on or picked over. They were watered enough to keep them alive, but many have had near-death experiences. If you had listened carefully, you would have heard them screaming: 'Get me out of here!' After Chelsea, planting out became a matter of urgency.

A few of our bedding plants became too pot-bound to thrive, but most recovered surprisingly well after some prompt treatment. In early June, we loaded one of the large trolleys – normally used for carting stacks of pots from the kiln – with crates of bedding plants and tender perennials, making sure that they'd all had a good soak beforehand. Then we set to work. We slashed solid balls of root in several places with a trowel to give an opening for new root growth from the centre. The ground was very dry this year, so the plants had to be watered in well. Such rescue work only succeeds if the plants are kept properly damp for several weeks while new roots break through into the surrounding earth.

Right: Andrew Lawson uses massed pots to create mini borders which he can experiment with and change round as the whim takes him. The results are always inspiring.

This year, we had trays of antirrhinums, sunflowers, *Cosmos bipinnatus*, *Cleome spinosa*, pot marigolds, French marigolds, *Cosmos sulphureus*, *Convolvulus tricolor* and *Anagallis monellii* to put out in any gaps. We do not agonise over colour schemes within our flowerbeds – we simply grow the flowers that we like, shoe-horn them in, sit back and enjoy the riot. Somehow it always works. The only people who complain about this horticultural incontinence are the potters, who find it harder and harder to find room to sit on the edges of the raised beds in the courtyard to drink their tea in the afternoon.

The bedding plants provide colour when the delphiniums and hardy geraniums peter out, and we keep a few gaps just big enough to take the fat, red dahlias that are the last to be hardened off outside the greenhouse. While we are in the borders, we stake the delphiniums as discreetly as possible with string and bamboo canes. These are the only plants that need staking early on, as their flower spikes shoot up in no time. In the circle garden next to my house, we put big stakes in for the tall polygonums and michaelmas daisies, the phlox, aconitum and *Lychnis chalcedonica*.

Early summer rain and warmth can accelerate growth so much that the tardy staker can be caught out. This year, however, the lack of natural and artificial irrigation has saved us some work, with many plants much shorter than they would be normally.

Once the bedding-out plants are gone, there is always a motley assortment left in the greenhouse of pelargoniums, argyranthemums and other tender perennials. These have been kept going over the years, many by cuttings, with some of the individual plants being several years old. A judge at a flower show would probably throw up his hands in horror at these contorted, leggy specimens, but we find them very useful for giving a planting instant maturity as they lean nonchalantly out of a pot or allow their lanky stems to be threaded through other plants.

Two different palettes of half-hardy plants. Facing page: Whichford in high summer, with verbenas, arctosis, *Felica ameilloides*, diascias, *Bidens ferulifolia* and *Alyogyne huegelii* 'Santa Cruz' in one frothy mass. Above: Kathy Brown's old swimming pool (see page 111) transformed by hot tropical colours with *Canna* 'Durban' to the fore.

In fact, when we tour nurseries looking for bigger plants for our displays we avoid the dense, bun-shaped ones that are churned out for big garden centres and supermarkets. Instead, we prefer the plants that Quality Control would certainly reject, as they are much easier to weave into a planting. We always keep a weather eye out for pests and pot-bound plants, which we spot by surreptitiously turning the plant upside down, removing the pot and inspecting its nether regions and by yellowing lower leaves.

Combining these old plants with other bought-in plants, such as petunias and the rejects from Chelsea, is great fun. Whether we feel like composing a symphony in blue and silver, shouting in purple, orange and red, or playing with shades of pink, there is room for all. It is wise, however, to keep the ultimate position of the plant in mind. Ferns, hostas, ivies and violas are happy against the north-west-facing wall of the pottery, but they would quickly scorch if placed in the south-facing triangular display space in the stockyard.

Left: A Sassanian jar sprayed with bronze centres a bed in the courtyard garden.
Above: A flared basket-weave pot echoes the sprays of phormium planted in it.
Below: The stunning shape of an aubergine plant, set off by a modern design.
Facing page: A planting returned from Chelsea fills a gap in the Paradise garden at Whichford.

Many bedding plants, such as *Lobelia erinus*, solenostemon and verbena, need plenty of sun to get going. They will last longer though, if they are then moved to a site that at least keeps the midday sun off them. You can cheat similarly with tulips and lilies – place their pots in a sunny position until they are just about to flower, so that they grow strong and upright, then put them in the shade just as their flowers are opening. That way, you can enjoy them for longer.

Plants such as *Gazania rigens* and *Pelargonium zonal* will take full sun and flower like mad, as long as they are watered occasionally. Of course, we break these rules all the time. We put ferns in with sun-loving osteospermums and pelargoniums and leave shade-loving *Tiarella cordifolia* in the sun because it is planted in a pot we want to display in the scorching open. But life and gardening would be so boring if you never bent any rules.

After a lunch sprawled in the shade, I drag myself drowsily back to the workshop. The pots are beginning to stiffen, and I toy with each one, always hoping for that perfect absolute. In throwing, this is seldom attainable, Yet the search for it tests skill and will, and sustains one's interest. I look glumly at my making list – it does include other pots that I could just about fit in, but they are not urgent, and it is so hot.

Left: A pot within a pot: the enduring image of the Tree of Life sprouting from an urn is embossed on to a tall, thin strip with a simple cockleshell imprint above and below.
Facing page: The ash-coloured texture on this pot is a perfect foil for the long trailing tresses of *Dichondra* 'Silver Falls' and *Ceropegia linearis* ssp 'Woodii' which hang down under the fleshy ears of *Kalanchoe tomentosa* and *K. beharensis*.

As if in answer to a prayer for deliverance, I notice my friend Paul Williams, plantsman and garden writer, sauntering down the path in sunhat and shorts, clutching a list. I wash my hands and go downstairs to meet him. He has come to borrow some pots for his book on planting design, and needs little persuasion to come and have a cold drink in the garden with me and talk gardening.

I have known Paul for many years, and have always enjoyed his combination of enthusiasm, knowledge and humour. He once gave a lecture at Whichford on pot plants, based on all the various species of the cannabis family in cultivation, rousing the somnolent after-lunch audience with a boisterous: 'Who here has smoked pot? Come on, now, no lying. Hands up!' Much hilarity ensued as various respectable-looking, middle-aged men were shopped by their wives for their flower-power student activities, and thereafter Paul had full attention for an erudite lecture.

Paul made his reputation for plantings as Head Gardener of Bourton House, in Gloucestershire. When he arrived, the garden was derelict, so he soon became a regular at the Women's Institute plant stalls in Moreton-in-Marsh. He'd buy up all their fuchsias, busy lizzies, and begonias, and stuff them into old terracotta lily pots which he had found in the greenhouse. It was a start that at least cheered up the drabbest corners.

But, above all, Paul is a plantsman. Show him a new plant and he is immediately hooked, noting its habits and talking through its likely family history. In particular, he loves tender perennials. 'Ask a gardener about some plant you ooh! and ah! over and it's always a tender perennial,' he says. 'They're just so exciting, aren't they, and effective right through the season.'

That been said, he has been quite rude about my Surfinias petunias. 'They're just over-performing little thugs, they'll swamp everything else!' And he hates big, blowsy fuchsias – why, I ask? 'Well, they're horrible!' he grins with a shrug of the shoulders. Species fuchsias are hastily excepted.

First in the list of restorations at Bourton House was the greenhouse, and soon it became home to a collection of his favourite tender perennials, all in hand-made flowerpots. Terracotta is always his first choice of material, partly because he is used to it

and partly because he values its weight as a counterbalance to the plants on a windy summer's day. He also loves the soft, neutral colour support that weathered terracotta gives to the plants.

However, he is not averse to coloured pots, or any other material that stimulates ideas for plantings. For example, the purchase of a couple of antique lead tanks gave Paul the space to play with new combinations from amongst his plant collection, and he found that he revelled in the greater dynamics possible. He also observed that big containers seemed to work better for the growth of the plants, presumably because of the increasing ratio of soil to surface area.

Above: A shallow, boat-shaped pot with a crew of echeveria, solenostemon and *Impatiens* 'Cranberry'.
Facing page: Paul Williams spotted this experimental pot at Whichford and rushed it off to his garden. There he planted it with the grass *Carex buchananii* and *Agastache* 'Apricot Sprite', setting it next to a border dominated by the same. The effect gives off almost electric energy.

colour theory

Above: Paul Williams shows his skill at combining plants, gravel and pot, dominated by a small corner of the colour spectrum. The result is a quiet harmony.

We talk about formulas for planting. Paul is always on the look out for ways to stretch compositions to the limit and, at the moment, he is particularly interested in height. Extreme plantings are one way of introducing a bit of humour (never far away with Paul) into the garden, although he stresses that quirky oddities only work if the composition that underpins them is good.

Paul sees the whole enterprise as an art. Every colour that the artist has is there for him, but living. This huge palette comes in every texture, from soft and fluffy to hard and shiny, and has to be balanced together with location and the shape of the chosen pot.

We get on to the subject of colour, wondering what will interest us next, and try to remember how our tastes have developed over the years. We soon come to the conclusion that attitudes are changing fast, but then that is nothing new.

If you go back to Medieval European gardens, colour, like so much else, could not be seen by an educated person simply for what it was, pleasing or not, but would primarily be read symbolically or allegorically. In the literature of the time, white stood for lilies or blossom, green for vines or grass, and red for roses. All these plants were laden with religious and amorous symbolism, frequently ambiguously and passionately intertwined.

The elegant white lily, for instance, was the special flower of Our Lady (the Madonna lily) with associations of virtue, purity and chastity. However, it was also highly desirable, ready to be picked, with a rich scent that enveloped one in dangerous sensuality. Green was seen as the colour of rebirth and everlasting life, the green of faith constantly renewed, but it was also the colour of primal, untamed nature, seen spewing from the mouths of Green Men all over Europe.

Balancing this rather intellectual approach was the underlying belief that contemplating natural beauty could lead to wisdom. According to an Anglo-Saxon proverb, 'Where we saw the flower of the lily, there we received the nectar of roses'. By the late Medieval period, it was realised that colour has a direct physical effect on those who see it. Thus, Hugh of Gouilloy, describing a cloister garth (the garden of a cloistered court), says that, 'The green turf which is in the middle of the material cloister refreshes encloistered eyes, and their desire to study returns. It is truly the nature of the colour green that it nourishes the eyes and freshens their vision.'

William of Auvergne attributed this restful and rejuvenating effect to the tonal value of green. It is neither black which dilates the eye, or white, which contracts it, but somewhere in between.

Below: Green and orange are separated on the colour wheel by yellow, and so offer each other a supportive contrast. Below right: Purple and blue lie next to each other on the wheel, so the eye is less sure of their relationship. Contrast of leaf shape, flower colour and the waving pennants of the pennisetum mediate.

The science of colour

It was not until the 19th century that the physical and psychological effect of colour began to be more scientifically studied. The most impressive work was done by the Frenchman, M Chevreul, who was director of the dye works at the famous Gobelins tapestry factory. After receiving repeated complaints from the design department that the colours he was supplying were fading, or not as bright as those that other companies were producing, he realised that part of the problem lay not with the colours of the threads, but with where they were put in relation to the overall colour scheme.

'I saw that the want of vigour alleged against the blacks was owing to the colours contiguous to them, and that the matter was involved in the phenomena of *the contrast of colours*.' By looking hard at the way colours reacted with each other, Chevreul was able to develop a Law of Simultaneous Contrast of Colours. He was soon applying the theory to every situation where colours impinge on each other, including horticulture.

Chevreul was perhaps the first to call the landscape gardener an artist. Over a period of more than 25 years, he gave lectures specifically to audiences of horticulturists, as well as others whose work involved making colour choices. A series of lectures given in Lyon were printed for the benefit of local designers and horticulturists, and a pirated version of these was translated and published in England soon after.

The 1859 English edition gives some idea of the huge scope of his interests, being titled *The Laws of Contrast of Colour: and their application to the arts of painting, decoration of buildings, mosaic*

Below: Red and purple are uncomfortably close colour neighbours, but are kept from fighting by the contrasting yellow border around the leaves of this solenostemon. With cross colouring in the other plants (red in the leaves of the fern and purple tinges in the lobelia) this becomes a quirky, but still slightly unsafe, planting.

work, tapestry and carpet weaving, calico printing, dress, paper staining, printing, illumination, landscape and flower gardening etc. The work included elaborate colour plates illustrating the effect of colours on each other and a planting plan for a landscape garden.

His bête noire was 'the ill effect produced by placing together many species of flower which, although of the same colour, are not of the same tint: for instance, in the spring we see the leopard's bane (doronicum), of a brilliant golden yellow, side by side with the narcissus, which is of a pale greenish yellow; in autumn, the Indian pink beside the African marigold, dahlias of various reds grouped together, &c. Such arrangements as these cause the eye, accustomed to appreciate the effects of contrast of colours, to feel sensations quite as disagreeable as those experienced by the musician whose ear is struck with discords.'

Below: The safe contrast between yellow and purply blue give this border a straightforward appeal, nicely focused by the open neck of an old amphora.

He thus advises against combinations of pink with scarlet and red, orange with orange-yellow, yellow with greenish-yellow, and blue with violet blue. 'I shall even go further in advising the separation of red flowers from orange, blue or pink from violet'. Only white avoids his censure: 'White flowers are the only ones that possess the advantage of heightening light tones of any colour, and of separating those whose colours are mutually injurious.'

Instead of these mutually injurious discords, he advocates planting colours together that are complementary to each other, giving mutually supportive contrast. This gives us the basis of the system that we recognise today as the colour wheel. It intersperses the three primary colours (not obtainable by the mixing together of any other colours) of red, blue and yellow, with the three secondary colours that lie in between them of purple, green and orange. The safest harmony of contrast is obtained by using colours that lie opposite each other on the wheel.

Gertrude's canvas

This pioneering work with colour was continued in the early 20th century by Gertrude Jekyll. Jekyll had studied as a painter and was inspired by the Impressionists, but poor eyesight eventually led her to abandon canvas for the garden. In her garden designs, she often used an old painting trick – the use of warm colours (saturated with red) to focus the eye, and the use of cool colours to give the impression of distance. To make a border wider or larger, hot colours were planted near the observer and cool ones far away.

In 1978, the Building Research Establishment in the UK published a remarkable study, based on the propositions of Chevreul and other colour theorists, to help co-ordinate the colours used in the manufacture of various materials. They concluded that the 'good taste' we associate with Jekyll and her school has a sound scientific base. Their main findings point to colour harmony as being a clear-cut, unambiguous relationship.

All-important is colour hue, rather than lightness or saturation. Colours of the same hue are harmonious, as are colours three to five steps apart (when the whole colour spectrum is divided into a 40-step scale). Also harmonious are those colours that provide a complete contrast (11 to 20 steps apart). They concluded that five was the maximum number of mutually harmonious hues; and that colour disharmony was always indefinite and ambiguous.

As a practical example, take the colour orange, which has a reputation for being difficult in the garden. According to this, an orange flower will be harmonious with another orange flower of exactly the same hue, an orange flower which is distinctly more red and an orange flower which is clearly more yellow. The orange would not look so good if the other oranges were too close in hue to our original flower – there needs to be some clear distinction between them. Neither would the orange look good if it was next to a very red purple or greeny yellow. However, these last two would be ideal candidates if you wanted a serious clash of colours. Also harmonious with our orange flower would be any blue from a purple blue to a greenish blue, although this would be the harmony of supportive contrast.

Right: A typical Great Dixter mixture of annuals grown in pots: the feisty orange of pot marigolds lifted by the contrasting blues of delphinium and campanula.

Harmony and contrast. Paul and I are not feeling at all scientific; however, we both agree that what we seek in our plantings is the excitement of colour contrasts, effects that wake up the eyes with a zing. A pause and we both mention Christopher Lloyd, who is fresh in my mind since I went to see him last week. His use of colour, indeed his whole gardening style, has had an enormous impact on all our tastes, not least because he writes about gardening so wittily, encouraging you to get out and try it for oneself.

Facing page: Christopher Lloyd likes to engineer pyramids of pots, those in the centre of the composition being raised on upturned empties. Most pots contain only single species, which allows him the freedom to adjust the composition easily as plants come in and out of season.

In *The Adventurous Gardener* he takes the refined good taste of mid-20th century gardening to task, saying that 'the trouble with the form-and-texture-and-colour-harmonies gardener is his (often her) insufferable self-consciousness'. The higher horticultural spheres, too, are often inhabited by prigs 'who choose progressively less gay plants, in contrast to the full-blooded vulgarity of suburban colour addicts who lurch incontinently from lumps of forsythia and double pink 'Kanzan' cherry, through a blaze of rhododendrons and dumpy blobs of azalea, floribunda roses, scarlet salvias and so to a dying exit with mop-headed chrysanthemums.'

Below: The famous oak-framed medieval porch at Great Dixter is always home to an ebullient amalgam of potted plants.

Christopher Lloyd's own garden at Great Dixter is a vibrant testimony to his insistence on mixing the rules of good taste with the full-blooded colours of a less refined palette. As I lifted the metal hook that fastens the bleached wooden gate leading into his garden, I did feel uncomfortably like a disciple. I have seen so many photographs and read so many articles about Great Dixter, but I soon found that the five hours I had allocated for the visit flashed past, and I still wanted to see more.

Great Dixter is a complex garden and each area has its own distinct feel. They are all informed, however, by the same eye. Plants with strong form and good foliage give a firm, year-round architectural structure, backed up by the marvellous outbuildings and hedges that enclose each garden. Colour is used in waves, with contrast harmonies punctuating the borders at strategic intervals between foliage plants. This illustrates Christopher's maxim that 'slabs of vivid colour with no company other than more slabs of vivid colour are exhausting, indigestible.'

Facing page: Spring at Great Dixter. Flowering aeoniums and brooms give a backdrop for spring bulbs, flanked by permanent plantings.
Above: The raised pond in the Whichford walled garden decorated with single-species plantings, including two different pink diascias and, at the back, two ornamental cabbages running gloriously to seed.

Colourful moods

The Building Research Establishment monograph talked scientifically about colour, but mentioned nothing about it inducing lassitude or stomach upset. Yet it does trigger a non-intellectual response. Elsewhere, Christopher says that 'blue is the flower colouring that most surely gets us, emotionally,' and a moment ago Paul was enthusing about orange. 'People fight shy of orange, but it fires you up!'

This is an altogether more subjective approach, ascribing different physiological or psychological effects to colour. Perhaps it is more akin to that medieval symbolism, when savants attributed colours to the virtues, the planets, days of the week. The Romantic Movement, too, leapt at this possible path to the emotions, although with much rivalry between theorists. 'If you hold a red cloth before a bull he will get furious, but if you as much as hint at colour the philosopher will go frantic,' said Goethe.

Below: Glaucous green leaves provide a calm setting for the more excitable red and orange tones.

Such disagreements still abound, and the New Age is a cornucopia of remarkable assertions on the effects of colour, sometimes held with alchemical fervour. One's choice of colour for plantings becomes disconcertingly revealing, and perhaps I should take more care with my own.

That yellow planting I did for instance – be warned: if you are afraid of being alone with your own thoughts, you may become caught up in the swirling waters of your mind as you look at it. Your blood pressure may increase and your respiration become uneven. You may break away from your usual attitudes and, with whirlwind intensity, seek adventure, romance and happiness amongst the yellow blooms.

Luckily, the greens in the garden should calm you down a bit – although if there is too much green it could lead you to a state of high anxiety combined with a desperate attempt to control trivialities. After all, 'the person who chooses green wants his opinions to prevail, to feel himself justified as a representative of basic and immutable principles… he puts himself on a pedestal and tends to moralise and to lecture others.' (Dr Max Lüscher in *The Lüscher Color Test*, 1970).

Overuse of purple is equally tricky, perhaps pointing to illusions of grandeur, and plunging the onlooker, after initial exhilaration, into irritable depression – Susan Lanman's 'malignant magenta'. On the other hand, Betty Wood, in *The Healing Power of Color*, 1984, states that lavender attracts creative types who 'hold elegant little parties where all the guests are very refined and cultivated'.

Dark blue seems to have a pacifying effect on the central nervous system. Its feminine 'mother' qualities giving a sense of belonging and safety. Rather oddly, Wood thinks this particularly suitable for lawyers, accountants and the overweight.

Red, of course, is the colour of strength and vitality, and is chosen by the vigorous, impulsive and aggressive. Lüscher states that it speeds up the pulse and raises blood pressure and breathing rate. It stands for all desires and cravings. Beware, however, when you shy away from those brash reds. Faber Birren in *Color and Human Response*, 1978, warns that 'if there is a dislike of red, which is fairly common, look for a person who has been frustrated, defeated

Above: Andrew Lawson gives a dead cherry tree the blues, but heats things up with lots of yellows and reds, and, of course, the orange of the flowerpots.

in some way, bitter and angry because of unfulfilled longings'. Almost as bad as pink types who, he feels, lack the courage to choose red to its full potential, and are frequently indulged dilettantes living in wealthy areas.

The more absurd theories aside, I am sure that colour does affect our mood, but people are very different in their responses. Age can also change our tastes. We are most colour-sensitive between the ages of 20 to 50, and blues may become less clear with age if the lenses of the eyes turn yellowish.

As he grew older, Monet increasingly used sharp notes of crimson red to focus his paintings of Giverny. In old age, he had a cataract operation, after which he was horrified to see such an abundance

of red, and his friends had great difficulty persuading him not to overpaint all his later oeuvre.

The flowerpot plantings at Great Dixter could never be accused of staying stuck in one mood, or even showing a preference for one colour. 'It's all very, very free, the same as the gardens', Fergus Garrett, Christopher's right-hand man, said to me, as I stood admiring his handiwork. 'You make mistakes, and sometimes they don't work, but if you don't allow that freedom, you are always going to play safe.' Or, as Christopher says, 'Our lives are bound by enough restrictions… the greater the range of plant materials that our gardening can assimilate without becoming an ill-assorted mess, the greater the satisfaction our hobby will afford us.' All sentiments with which I heartily agree.

a mix-and-match approach

Paul Williams and I both love multi-species plantings in big pots. At Great Dixter, Christopher and Fergus have quite a different way of using diverse plant material. They plant large numbers of 18 to 30cm (7 to 12in) pots with single species. These are then grouped together in a large mass, those in the middle raised up on upturned pots. Most of the pots are covered by the mass of plants, with only the shallow pans at the edges of the arrangement showing.

Arranging these pots usually takes Fergus several hours as he goes back and forth to the nursery collecting and trying out different plant combinations. Sometimes, it is only a few flowering annuals that need replacing – Fergus pointed out the cornflowers that were going over when I was there – in which case the other pots will only be adjusted. However, every month or so everything is dismantled and rebuilt from scratch to incorporate new plants and colours.

Sometimes the biggest and central plants stay put all season. The banana to the left of the main porch, grown from a seed in Fergus's lunchbox, is this year's favourite, its fronds spreading over the plants below. It also looks extraordinary framed by medieval beams as you come out of the porch. The light from the outside filters luminous green through the dark skeleton of its ribs.

For this kind of gardening, where annual and tender bedding plants are changed twice or even three times a year, a back-up area containing a big range of plants for bedding and pots is essential. Fergus took me down to the nursery that grows plants for sale and for use in the gardens. First we passed through an enclosed courtyard with beds around its walls, paved with a mosaic of stones and tiles depicting Christopher's two dachschunds, Dahlia and Canna. A grouping of flowerpots spreads out on top of their paws.

At Great Dixter, Christopher Lloyd and Fergus Garrett are constantly experimenting with composition. Canna and turk's cap lilies form a backdrop for several kinds of begonia and the tall white spikes of *Francoa sonchifolia* (facing page). Canna and turk's cap remain the same, but on the other side of the entrance porch they are partnered with yellow argyranthemum and orange gaillardia (right).

Through an arch, and at the bottom of the steps in front of you is another group, and yet another beside it, each one quite different. One has red, blue, yellow, white, silver, purple, pink and green. Another has orange, light blue, dark blue, red and pink. What of colour theory? 'I have no segregated colour schemes. In fact, I take it as a challenge to combine every sort of colour effectively,' says Fergus.

Down in the nursery, we looked at two large Whichford pots recently planted up. They will not be allowed out on public display until they knit up and conform to the Great Dixter dictum of 'no bare soil'. Christopher worries about the difficulty of moving around pots of this size, but they do give him the chance to do a few multi-species plantings. They will end up used as tall centrepieces surrounded by the characteristic medley of other plantings. The whole will look like some extravagant experimental flower arrangement that uses living plants rather than cut.

the lone rangers

At Whichford, despite our preference for multi-species plantings, we do also use single-species plantings. Often this is because of a plant's domineering habits – even our hostas do not seem to like sharing a pot. There are also those plants that are appealing but unruly and need the discipline provided by life in a pot. Many grasses and bamboos suddenly seem much more attractive when there is no chance that they will march across your lawn.

We use *Euphorbia griffithii* 'Fireglow' in a permanently planted pot and it obligingly throws up its brightly coloured shoots every year – you never know exactly where in the planting it is going to emerge. *Lamium maculatum* and *Ajuga reptans* (and all their variations) become quite well-mannered in a pot and display qualities of leaf colour that go unnoticed when they are mere ground-cover.

In harder cases, we use pots as prisons for wayward plants. All varieties of mint are sentenced, and it is the best way to control the thuggish *Vinca* brothers (*major* and *minor*) who prove very useful in winter plantings, although they make persistent attempts at escape. The variegated ground elder *Aegopodium podagraria* 'Variegatum' should not be trusted either and, next year, we may sentence some *Acanthus spinosus* to a term in the slammer. There are many more plants out there that may benefit from this treatment. Some will not thrive, or will rush to the edge of the pot and stare sadly out, but for many it is the ideal way to repay their debt to gardening society.

After Christopher's colour iconoclasm, Paul and I wonder if there are any rules left to guide us. For me, the theories of colour harmony definitely work to create pleasing effects. Yet they need to be used in their contrasting combinations often enough to prevent blandness, and I cannot promise that there will not be the occasional horrible clash waiting to seize you around the next corner.

Some plants just do not need partners. Hostas (above, centre) grow best alone, out of the way of slugs, and the forms of asphodel (above, right) and aloe (below, centre) easily hold their own. The variegated mint (below, right) is enough to fill a green-glazed longtom, and who could want more than the mound of *Viola* 'Jackanapes' (below, left). Some pots are best left single too, like this dark experiment (above left).

rhythm and structure

Great Dixter also reminds me that structure is just as important to a planting as colour. Leaf shape and texture need to be balanced. It is often the contrast of thin and spiky with curvy and rounded that catches the eye, or the surprise of noticing smooth and shiny emerging from beneath soft and frizzy.

Above all, to be successful a planting must have rhythm. The eye must be led around by shape and colour and then be given some focal point upon which to come to rest. In this sense, flowerpot planting is no different from all gardening.

Reluctantly, Paul and I draw our conversation to a close – we both have work to do. I leave him to choose the pots that he needs, and go on through the pottery garden to tramp up the back stairs. I walk along the balcony that hangs over the clay pile, now dry and cracked, the three raw clays each their own, distinct colour, and head into the throwing workshop.

My two pots are still gyrating slowly on their wheels and are noticeably drier. I meticulously measure the height of a decorative band, drawing a line around the pot onto which I squeeze soft clay. I form it with a wet sponge – perhaps I should try a chamois leather like my Italian friends – and finish the details with the fingernail of my little finger.

I call for help and four of us grunt and heave the third section of each pot into place. I fettle the joins and then ease out the new parts until they follow the growing line of the pots. That is enough for today. Tomorrow, we will add the rims (the fourth sections) and, in three or four days, the great lions' heads that hang from the sides will need to be luted on. But that is all we can do safely today.

You can sense the relief as the working day nears its end. I have a last couple of kiln duties, watching until, with much hissing and throbbing, the whole interior of the kiln and its load pulsate with the

Below: The simple, solid form of a group of longtoms is in beautiful contrast to the cloud grass, *Agrostis nebulosa*.

colour of shining straw. Then, the pots are cooked, and I, too will be finished. It is so hot as I pass between the two big kilns that I can hardly breathe.

Tonight we will be all meeting up again – this heat may not be so good for work, but it is excellent for parties in the garden. Richard will swap his clay-smattered overalls for an apron and become the barbecue chef. Everyone will bring their contributions, Issy with some delicacy to delight us all. We will sit in the courtyard, surrounded by our pots, and chatter about the day just past, while drinking toasts as the evening light comes slanting through the arches.

As the air becomes cooler and the wine flows, we will relax into the languorous scents of the sweet tobacco plants, lavenders and lilies growing all about us. The magentas and reds will start to glow, and the white will shine luminous for the moths that hover in the gathering dusk.

In the summer we are spoilt for choice, especially in some genera, such as *Hosta* and *Pelargonium* – so here is just a selection of regulars.

Hardy perennials

Actaea racemosa **F; T**

Anchusa azurea 'Loddon Royalist' **H** (trim after flowering)

Aquilegia chrysantha **S–PS**

Athyrium niponicum var. *pictum* **F; PS–Sh**

Foeniculum vulgare **F; S; WD**

Hosta – many, many species and varieties **F; PS–Sh; R**

Penstemon **S; WD**

Salvia nemorosa 'Ostfriesland' **S–PS; R**

Stachys byzantina **F; H**

Tiarella cordifolia **F; Sh**

Tolmiea menziesii **F; Sh**

Bulbs

Allium vineale **H; T**

Camassia leichtlinii **S–PS**

Galtonia candicans **S; T; WD**

Lilium – many, eg 'Black Beauty' **P; S–PS; WD**

L. regale **P; S–PS; WD**

L. speciosum var. *rubrum* **E; S–PS; WD**

Alpines/miniatures

Helianthemum nummularium **H; WD**

Lewisia cotyledon **E; H**

Lithodora diffusa **E; S**

Origanum 'Kent Beauty' **M; S; T**

Parahebe catarractae

Phlox adsurgens 'Wagon Wheel' **E; PS; R**

P. divaricata **E; PS; R**

Semiaquilegia ecalcarata **T**

Evergreen shrubs

Cistus x *purpureus* **H; WD**

Hebe pinguifolia 'Pagei' **F; H**

Lavandula angustifolia **H; P; WD** (shear off flower spikes after flowering)

Rosmarinus officinalis **H; P; WD**

Salvia officinalis 'Purpurascens', 'Tricolor' **F; H; P; WD**

Deciduous shrubs

Abutilon vitifolium **S; WD**

Hibiscus syriacus **R; S; WD**

Tender perennials

Abutilon megapotamicum **S; WD**

Aeonium 'Zwartkop' **F; S; T**

Agapanthus africanus **H; M**

A. campanulatus **H**

Agave americana 'Variegata' **F; H; WD**

Argyranthemum 'Jamaica Primrose', 'Qinta White', 'Vancouver' **S; WD**

Brugmansia x *candida* **P; S**

Convolvulus cneorum **F; H; M**

C. sabatius **H; M**

Cuphea cyanaea **S; WD**

C. llavea 'Tiny Mice' **S; T; WD**

Diascia 'Snowdrift' **S; WD**

Dicksonia antarctica **F; PS–Sh; R; T**

Echeveria **F; H; T; WD**

Felicia amelloides **S; WD**

Gazania **H; WD**

Helichrysum petiolare **F; H**

Heliotropium arborescens **P**

Lantana camara **S–PS; WD**

Lavandula dentata **F; H; P**

Lotus berthelotii **F; S; T; WD**

Osteospermum 'Silver Sparkler' **H**; 'Whirlygig' **H; T**

Pelargonium (ivy-leaved) 'Barbe Bleue' **H**; 'L'Elégante' **F; H**

P. (regal) 'Lord Bute' **T**

P. (scented leaf) 'Atomic Snowflake', *P. crispum* 'Variegatum', 'Lady Plymouth', *P. tomentosum* **F; H; P**

Pelargonium zonal – many varieties **H**

Salvia corrugata **F; M**

S. leucantha **H; M**

S. microphylla **M**

S. patens 'Cambridge Blue' **T**

S. semiatrata **T**

Senecio cineraria 'Silver Dust' **F; M; S**

Tradescantia pallida 'Purpurea' **F; R; S–PS; T; WD**

Annuals and bedding plants

Most annuals and bedding plants like a sunny site and well-drained soil.

Antirrhinum majus **Se**

Asarina erubescens **Se**

Begonia (tuberous and semperflorens) **PS–Sh; R**

Bidens ferulifolia

Brachyscome iberidifolia

Calendula officinalis **Se**

Cerinthe major 'Purpurascens' **F; Se; T**

Cobaea scandens **Se; T**

Cosmos sulphureus **Se**

Impatiens **Sh**

Ipomoea tricolor 'Heavenly Blue' **H; Se**

Lathyrus odoratus 'Cupani', 'Painted Lady' **P; Se**

L. sativus **Se; T**

Lobelia erinus **Se**

Mimulus 'Magic Series' **R**

Nemesia

Nemophila menziesii 'Pennie Black' **T**

Nicotiana alata **P; Se; Sh**

Solenostemon (especially reddish-purple ones, such as 'Etna') **F; Sh**

Tagetes 'Jolly Jester', 'Vanilla' **Se**

Tropaeolum majus **Se**

Verbena (many – Tapien varieties are good) **S–PS**

Key

E: Prefers ericaceous compost

F: Interesting foliage

H: Tolerates a baking hot position

M: Survives mild winters outside with good drainage but take insurance cuttings first!

P: Scented foliage or flowers

PS–Sh: Thrives in partial shade or shade

R: Likes a rich, fertile soil (add organic matter, such as leaf-mould)

S: Prefers a sunny site

Se: We usually grow this from seed sown in spring

S–PS: Will tolerate sun or partial shade

S–Sh   Happy with either sun or shade

Sh: Thrives in a shady position

T: Talking-point/attention-grabber – people will ask you what that plant is!

WD: Requires a very well-drained soil that includes added grit or coarse sand.

Above: White verbenas shine out of their supporting foliage plants, purple sage and glaucous *Convolvulus cneorum*. The swirling decoration on the pot is taken from pre-Islamic Persian pottery.

Below: My twelve-year-old son Columba's choice of plants, showing what fun children can have with pots, especially one like this wise head, made by another Whichford potter, Anne Townly.

Acknowledgements

All photographs by Andrew Lawson except the following, arranged alphabetically:

Key: t = top; b = bottom; l = left; r = right
Page 132 akg-images / Erich Lessing; 23(x2) Antiquarian Images; 25, 45, 123, 138(t), 149(b), 169(tr) Elly Crook; 113, 114(l), 115(l), 149(tl), 168(b), 169(tl,bl) Liz Eddison; 42 Christa Holm; 2, 7, 8, 9, 12, 13, 14, 16(rx3), 17(x3), 26, 35 (tl,tr,br), 41, 43, 48, 49, 51, 54–55, 59, 64, 66(r), 67, 69, 74, 76, 78, 79(l), 88(r), 91, 94, 106–107, 109 (tl,br,bl), 112, 114(r), 121(bl), 124, 125(x2), 126, 127, 128, 129, 130(tl), 131(bl), 138(b), 141(tr), 142, 158–159, 164, 168(t), 169(br), 173(b) Jim Keeling; 133 Pots and Pithoi; 60 The Stapleton Collection / Bridgeman Art Library

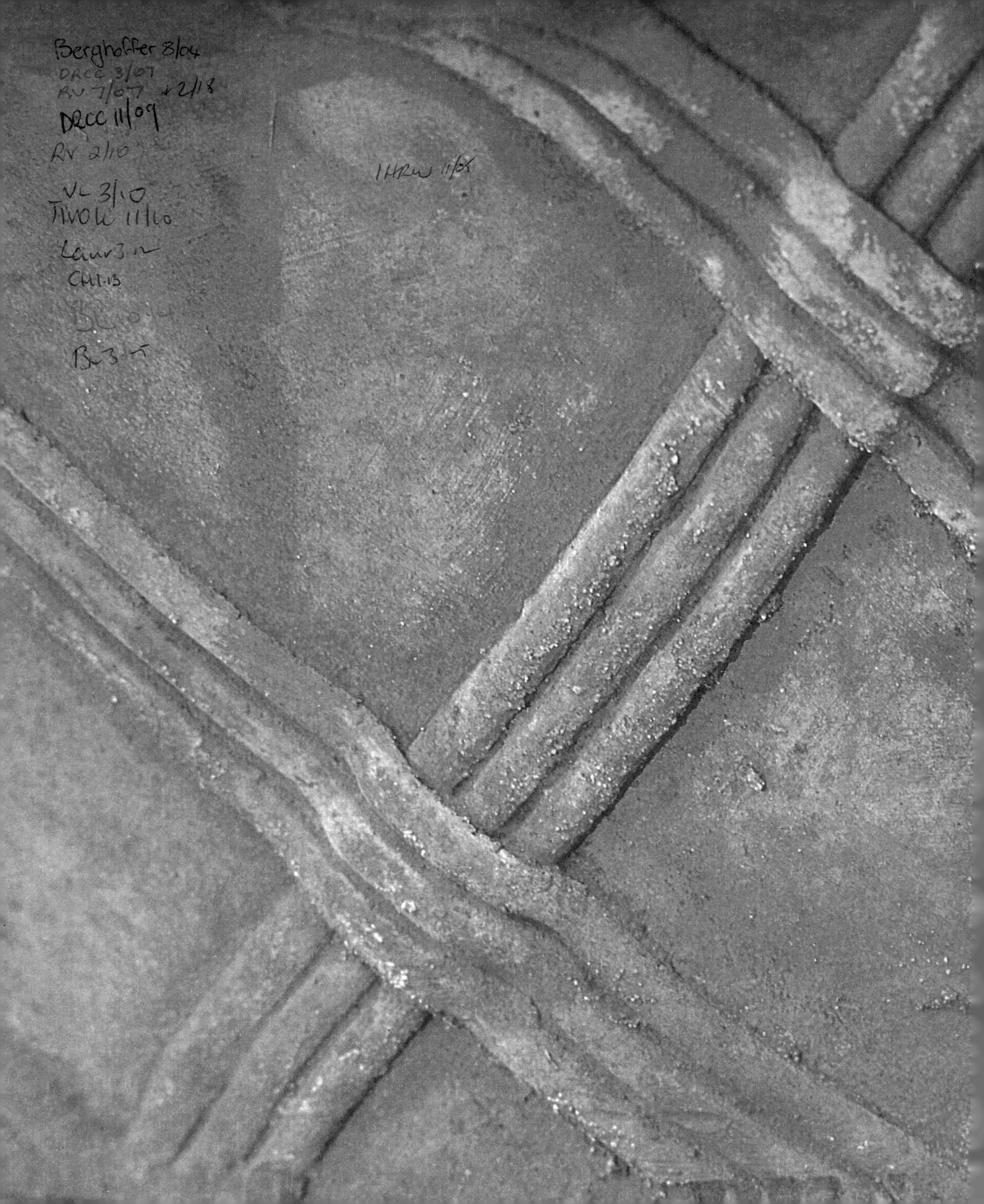
Berghoffer 8/04
DRCC 3/07
DRCC 11/09